KANDINSKY	**ERNST**
LÉGER	**DELAUNAY**
BRAQUE	**PICASSO**
MONDRIAN	**POLLOCK**
KLEE	**KLINE**
MIRÒ	**DE KOONING**

THE WORK OF THESE and many other outstanding painters who have created our contemporary art is engagingly and intelligently discussed by an eminent authority, Michel Seuphor. The various 'isms' — Suprematism, Futurism, Rayonism, Purism, Dadaism, to mention a few — are described, their manifestoes are quoted, and the contributions and influence of each are pointed out. Seen through Mr. Seuphor's eyes, the entire movement — seemingly so complex and confusing to the amateur of art — appears to follow a pattern.

Over 100 reproductions of the 20th-century masterpieces both in color and black-and-white provide the reader with a fuller understanding and appreciation of this art of our century.

ALSO AVAILABLE IN

LAUREL EDITIONS

———

ART TREASURES OF THE LOUVRE

by René Huyghe

MODERN AMERICAN PAINTING AND SCULPTURE

by Sam Hunter

MODERN FRENCH PAINTING

by Sam Hunter

Abstract

Painting

50 YEARS OF

ACCOMPLISHMENT,

FROM

KANDINSKY

TO THE PRESENT

TEXT BY MICHEL SEUPHOR

A LAUREL  *EDITION*

Published by

DELL PUBLISHING CO., INC.

750 Third Avenue

New York 17, N.Y.

Library of Congress Catalog Card Number: 61-15924

Laurel (R) TM674623, Dell Publishing Co., Inc.

Translated from the French by Haakon Chevalier

First Dell Printing 1964

Printed in Holland   Smeets Photo-offset Weert Holland

ACKNOWLEDGMENTS

The successful creation of an artbook must have the close collaboration of publisher, printer, and author. This is basic. But a book which deals exclusively with contemporary art depends more than most on the friendly cooperation of private collectors, museums of modern art, and art dealers. Thus, I am anxious to convey here my gratitude to all those who have helped so willingly in my complex undertaking. Particularly I want to thank M. François Arp, Mme J. Arp-Hagenbach, Mr. John Craven, Mme G. Dupin, M. Pierre Peissi, M. Jacques Putman, all of Paris. I am much obliged to the Musée National d'Art Moderne, Paris, and to the following Parisian galleries: Ariel, Charpentier, Claude Bernard, Creuze, Denise René, Creuzevault, Daniel Cordier, Drouin, Dubourg, Europe Philadelphie, Flinker, de France, Jacques Massol Jeanne Bucher, Kléber, Knoedler, La Hune, Louis Carré, Louise Leiris, Maeght, Pierre, Rive-Droite, Villand and Galanis, XXème Siècle, and the Galerie Internationale d'Art Contemporain. Thanks go also to Mr. and Mrs. Burton G. Tremaine of Meriden, Connecticut; to Mrs. Kay Hillman, Dr. and Mrs. Arthur Lejwa, and Mrs. Silvia Pizitz of New York; to Mr. and Mrs. Henry A. Markus of Chicago; to Mr. and Mrs. Herbert M. Rothschild of Ossining, New York; to Mr. and Mrs. Harry L. Winston of Birmingham, Michigan; to the Museum of Modern Art, New York; to the Solomon R. Guggenheim Museum, and the Whitney Museum of American Art in New York; to the Philadelphia Museum of Art; and the following New York galleries: André Emmerich, Betty Parsons, Leo Castelli, Chalette, Kootz, Martha Jackson, and Sidney Janis; to the Esther Robles Gallery in Los Angeles. In Europe, to Dr. Wolfgang Macke; to the Städtische Galerie of Munich; the Kaiser Wilhelm Museum of Krefeld; the Staatliche Kunsthalle in Karlsruhe; the Städtisches Kunsthaus of Bielefeld; the Galerie Der Spiegel in Cologne; the Galerie Otto Stangl in Munich; the Print Room in Vienna; the Musée d'Art Moderne in Brussels. In England, to Mr. Roland Penrose and Mr. E. J. Power of London; the Tate Gallery, London; and the London galleries of art: Arthur Tooth & Sons, Gimpel fils, and Lord's. In Milan, the Galleria d'Arte Moderna, and the following art galleries: Cardazzo, Lorenzelli, and Schwarz In Holland, the Stedelijk Museum, Amsterdam; Gemeentemuseum, The Hague; the Kröller-Müller Museum, Otterlo. In Switzerland, M. Alberto Sartoris of Lutry; the Galerie Lienhard, Zurich; the Galerie Beyeler, Basel. I must also mention the courtesies of many artists and close relatives of artists.

Especially I would like to thank the designer of the book, Ben Duijvelshoff, for his devoted attention to every detail of the presentation.

M.S

PART ONE

Before 1915

Our twentieth-century world, with its swift technological and scientific advances and socio-economic upheavals, our century which has witnessed the rapid shrinking of the world's dimensions, was obligated to give its children an art which reflected these changes. Yet today the average man in the street (who may occasionally be led to cast a casual glance in the direction of artistic creation) still sees abstract art as a visual experience and mental challenge that is both revolutionary and startling — a form of art at times both irritating and aggressive, and at other times meaningless or merely innocuous and inoffensive. We know, of course, how disconcerting such impressions can be. But the experienced observer, with his practiced eye, has an altogether different perspective; for him surprises are rare, everything is related, nothing manifests itself which has not been foreshadowed. Yet the fact remains that the artistic evolution peculiar to each century, to each generation (and in fact to each truly original artist), is such that developments nevertheless occur contrary to the most clearsighted prognostications. For while the general direction of the movement may be well known to us, any move is composed of a host of small accidents, which are unforeseeable and which may cause the movement's direction to swerve, to falter, and even, for a time, to change its course. Because of this uncertainty there is a certain element of surprise, no matter how close and attentive the witness may be.

Balzac and Baudelaire prophesied abstract art in their writings; the Impressionists, Post-Impressionists, and Fauves celebrated it in bold words, although apparently without quite knowing what they were saying, since none of them practiced what he preached. The Cubists at last resolutely ventured into this new territory, but despite the brilliance of their works they immediately drew back. They were to return to it, if their names happened to be Delaunay or Villon, only much later; Braque and Picasso never returned. No, this territory which today appears so immense — a kind of promised land — was not to belong to the Cubists, however great; they sensed the emptiness. The renunciation of figurative art seemed to mortally imperil their youth, and they had too many flavors still to discover in the traditional values. Thus it was the older painters who first staked out the new territory and settled there for good: Mondrian was forty in 1912, Kupka forty-one, and Kandinsky forty-six.

Since its beginnings in 1912, the multiplicity of forms of expression has been one of the most singular characteristics of abstract painting. When we measure the distance traveled and the enormous present-day expansion of this art and then go back to the tiny core of artists working in 1912 we discover, not without amazement, that all the basic elements were already present at the start in the combined works of Kupka, Kandinsky, and Delaunay. The rectangular and horizontal-vertical style can be found in certain canvases of Kupka's of 1912; lyric effusiveness is the very essence of Kandinsky's work at this period, and some of these early paintings could be called *tachiste* or nonformal if they had been painted in 1960. Finally Delaunay contributed order and wisdom in a style rich with a kind of inner vibration. In his paintings, light is composed rather like a well-balanced musical work, to which the painter accords just the right amount of required warmth, without ever being carried away or dominated by it. Before such accomplished works of this first period, one is tempted to say that, with these men, art reached a destination rather than a point of departure. This statement, however, would overlook the uncontrollable factor of each individual and the unpredictable scope of his work. The art of the century had yet to *find itself*, there was a style to be created and a universal form to develop, there was a need to overcome the violent opposition of traditionalist circles, there was a war to face, a faith in their work to affirm. In short, it was necessary to create history with what was yet contained within the seed.

What this seed of 1912 contained was going to spread throughout the world and to manifest both its revolutionary character (as a wrenching loose from the naturalism of the last century) and the fundamental outgiving of its multiple nature. This multiplicity itself belonged to the spirit of the century: modern man, even more than man in the age of Montaigne, is "changeable and diverse." If he is truly unconstrained, nothing is so repellent to him as rigidity of attitudes. This multiplicity is above all an expression of the richness of the spirit, it is passionate, and at the same time open and flexible, having nothing in common with the eclecticism of the blasé collector or the dilletante aesthete. It is a sign of love, of overflowing abundance.

At the root of this multiplicity there is a certain conception of reality, a specific conception of existence and of the values it contains. Matisse once said, "We are born with the sensibility of a period of civilization. We are not masters of our production, it is imposed upon us." This at once appears self-evident. The difficulty begins when we try to define this sensibility — a sensibility peculiar to our epoch and which inevitably determines our selves. For we soon discover that there are as many distinct sensibilities as there are great artists. When I compare the styles of Mondrian, Arp, Delaunay, Kandinsky, Mirò, Schwitters, Ernst, Herbin, Picasso, and Matisse, the only common denominator I can find is that none of them can be made to fit into the nineteenth century. The painting's frame, or the background on which it hangs, remains. But against this background, or within this frame, individualism remains dominant, perhaps more so today than ever before.

As early as 1909, the Cubist painters destroyed the object and reconstructed it in a different way, improvising freely with pictorial means and without taking objective reality into account. In so doing, they implicitly discovered the uselessness of the object and, in fact, proved themselves, to be the first creators of abstract painting.

Their logic was such that they did not entirely repudiate the object, even though they refused to be dominated by it. As a consequence, no holds were barred in this wrestling match, in this new love-game between the object and painting as such, a game in which the actual object soon became the pictorial technique itself. With the Impressionists, as we know, technique was no less important; but a landscape always had to remain a landscape, the ideal painting being the one that would succeed in giving the viewer the direct impressions of the painter's retina. The "how" never had priority over the "what."

The opposite is true of Cubism. The nudes and the still lifes by Braque and Picasso (in the latter's great period) make no effort to be recognizable as such. These works ask the viewer to consider only the elements of painting as painting, and they ask him to derive his sole enjoyment from these elements. As a result, the "what" is absorbed by the "why."

Even more than the destruction of the object, the desire to construct, from simple pictorial elements of a generally rectilinear nature, is manifest in all the Cubists, and thus Constructivism is very clearly foreshadowed in their canvases. All that was needed was to enlarge the detail, and to discover in this magnification the tension and the *relationships* of the lines. We shall see, further on, the importance this concept of relationships assumed for Mondrian, who was to make it one of the essential foundations of his logic.

For the moment we shall limit ourselves to noting that there was, between 1906 and 1914, a widespread simultaneity of discovery throughout Europe, in the realm of thought as well as in that of the plastic arts and poetry, a general atmosphere of birth to which Guillaume Apollinaire, a little later, entitled *l'esprit nouveau*.

Something had its beginning when Kandinsky, returning to his studio at twilight one day, was surprised to see a canvas "of an indescribable and incandescent beauty" which he did not at once recognize as his own, because it had been placed on its side; something had its beginning when Kupka, in the course of a walk, apologized to nature for having attempted to copy it and promised not to do so again; something had its beginning when Marinetti published the "Manifesto of Futurism" in *Le Figaro* in 1909; something had its beginning when Mondrian wrote in his sketchbook: "The surface of things gives enjoyment, their interiority gives life"; something had its beginning when Robert Delaunay painted his first *Window Open on the City*, which allowed light to break into the canvas with its entire range of the spectrum; something had its beginning when in 1913, Marcel Duchamp and Francis Picabia went to New York to preach the gospel of a new art and were the great attraction of the Armory Show; something had its beginning when Brancusi, weary of "making corpses," conceived the *Sleeping Muse*, which was gradually to become transformed into a simple ovoid; something had its beginning when there was nothing.

It was then that Kandinsky, in Munich, uttered the well-known words: "Everything is permitted" *(alles ist erlaubt)*. In 1961, we still live by this heritage, which in truth is inexhaustible.

The year 1912 will always remain the turning point for the art of this century. Cubism was at its apogee, and Mondrian was learning from it in Paris, where he had come in the last days of 1911. He soon went beyond it and through his first works, although still Cubist, arrived at his Neo-Plastic law of the right angle. In February, Severini and the Futurists exhibited at Bernheim's. In April, at the Salon des Indépendants, among other new magnitudes of painting, there could be seen Delaunay's *Simultaneous Windows* and Marcel Duchamp's *Nude Descending a Staircase*. Gris, just beginning to be recognized, exhibited in the Salon for the first time. In March, Gleizes and Metzinger published *Du Cubisme*. October saw the first show of the *Section d'Or* ("The Golden Section") at the Galerie de la Boëtie, with more than two hundred works, among which were Picabia's *Les danseuses à la source (The Dancers at the Fountain)* and a series of wholly abstract works by Kupka together with the paintings of nearly all the other Cubists including, of course, the three Duchamp brothers who initiated this enormous undertaking. At the Salon d'Automne, Kupka exhibited his *Fugue à deux couleurs (Fugue in Two Colors)* and *Chromatique chaude (Warm Chromatic Scale)*, and also Duchamp-Villon's frontal plan for the "Cubist house."

1   Morgan Russell • *Sketch from a Notebook* • 1912

In Munich, Kandinsky published his theoretical work, *Über das Geistige in der Kunst (On the Spiritual in Art)* which cast light upon the *Almanach* and the exhibitions by the Blaue Reiter group. Finally, Berlin saw the first exhibits of the Der Sturm Gallery, named for the famous review that championed the cause of Expressionism (later for abstract art also) which Walden had been editing since 1910. Among the gallery's exhibitors, during its first months, were to be found names new to Berlin: Braque, Picasso, Herbin, Delaunay, Arp, Reth, Severini, and Archipenko, together with more familiar names to Berliners: Kokoschka, Jawlensky, Kandinsky, Marc, and Campendonck. In the realm of the arts the time was propitious, and no war threatened. Two years later, at the very outbreak of the First World War (which put an abrupt stop to those brotherly associations and exchanges) the Sturm Gallery exhibited the works of Gleizes, Metzinger, Villon, Duchamp-Villon, and Marc Chagall.

Delaunay and Léger introduced bright color into the Cubist grayness, the former by his swirling rhythms, the latter by his contrasting forms. Previous to this, Delaunay had set himself with passion to painting and drawing the Eiffel Tower. The Tower, so reviled by academic poets, was suddenly acclaimed by a new generation of poets, with Apollinaire in the lead. It, too, needed its portraitist. The Tower symbolizes the virility of Paris, and at the same time its grace: groom and bridal veil, abundance and charm in the same symbol. We owe Delaunay our blessings for having glorified the Eiffel Tower as early as 1910, as well as for having immediately broken it to bits, so as to prove that painting is and must be free.

The Tower keeps reappearing in Delaunay's painting, whole

and in many fragments. At times its presence is only faintly suggested, as a mere grid of lines in the middle of an abstract composition.

However, it is the circular rhythms, together with the effects of simultaneous contrast, that are strikingly important in Delaunay's work. Beyond a doubt, for the first time in the history of art, color is displayed for its own sake: it sings for the sake of singing, and vibrates for the sake of vibrating, without the slightest naturalist context. In his sometimes confused notes on painting, Delaunay tries to explain his debt to Seurat, and how he differs from the Divisionists who employ color contrasts to intensify the vision of nature for the viewer. To him the law of complementaries serves as both the foundation and the object of his art. To make this point more explicit, Delaunay enlarges, to unprecedented dimensions, the motifs that had been subordinated by the Divisionists. In much the same way the earliest Constructivists seemed to be amplifying fragments of paintings by Braque and Picasso.

The painting of light having become an end in itself, we grasp why Delaunay was so attracted by the solar disk. His works are full of allusions to celestial events. There is no painting at once so close to poetry and yet so much "pure painting" as Delaunay's. Nor is there any painting more cosmic in conception. We can hardly be surprised that Apollinaire should have dubbed it "Orphic." It may well have been Delaunay's art which inspired him to declare: "I love the art of today because I love light above all else. For man, who invented fire, loves light above all else."

It was Apollinaire, too, who said that Delaunay's swirling rhythms were "the first manifestation of non-objective art in France, that is, of an art proceeding not from an external subject, but from an internal subject."

Sonia Delaunay followed her husband's painting and ideas very closely, more like a colleague than a disciple, and this is proved by her well-accomplished works such as *Electric Prisms* (1914) and *Bal Bullier* (1913).

Fernand Léger's contrasting forms of 1913 and 1914 introduced into the Cubist climate an element of lightness and of improvisation which it had not yet known. His treatment was altogether sketchy, the surface only partly covered, yet no one could deny that the canvas was well-filled and prodigiously animated. Leger's was a very supple form of pure painting, rich with far-reaching anticipations. According to a statement made by Léger in Montjoy in 1913, this conception of painting "is not a passing abstraction, good only for a few initiates," but "the total expression of a new generation whose necessities it experiences and to all of whose aspirations it constitutes a response."

As we know, Léger soon abandoned this direction in favor of heavier painting into which, about 1921, he introduced the human figure — a figure sketchily drawn, to be sure, but whose contours were singularly soft. Yet the problems of abstract painting continued to absorb him. He returned to these problems, in a series of mural paintings done in 1924, visibly influenced by Mondrian. I was seeing a good deal of Léger during those years, and he would question me time and again about Mondrian. While these questions betrayed a certain anxiety, he would usually end the conversation with some quip to the effect that "These Northerners always carry things too far." I never contradicted him. But it has since become clear to me how important it is to carry things too far. The world would stand still if no one ventured beyond the limits of the familiar. Such small advances as we make, despite the inertia that holds

2   Georges Braque • *Woman Reading* • 1911

3 Georges Braque • *Violin and Pipe* • 1912

4 Pablo Picasso • *Bottle, Glass, and Violin* • 1912-13

5   Robert Delaunay • *Simultaneous Disk* • 1912

6   Juan Gris • *Still Life with Pears* • 1913

7   Robert Delaunay • *Circular Forms* • 1912-13

8   Sonia Delaunay • *Electric Prisms* • 1914

9   Michel Larionov • *Rayonism* • 1911

10   Giacomo Balla • *Little Girl Running on a Balcony* • 1912

11   Marcel Duchamp • *Nude Descending a Staircase* No 2 • 1912

12   Jacques Villon • *Soldiers on the March* • 1913

13   Piet Mondrian • *Apple Trees in Bloom* • 1912

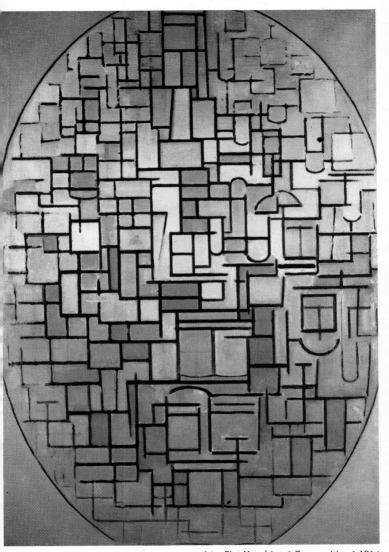

14   Piet Mondrian • *Composition* • 1914

15 Wassily Kandinsky • *Deluge I* • 1912

16 Wassily Kandinsky • *All Saints' Day* • c. 1910-11

17   Wassily Kandinsky • *With the Black Arch* • 1912

18   Frank Kupka • *Arrangement in Yellow Verticals* • 1912-13

19   Frank Kupka • *Disks* • 1911-12

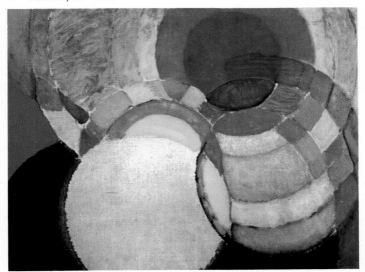

20   Fernand Léger • *Contrast of Forms* • 1913

21   Stanton Macdonald-Wright • *Synchromy* • 1914

22   Kasimir Malevich • *The Guard* • 1912-14

23   Kasimir Malevich • *Supreme* • Before 1915

24 Francis Picabia • *Rubber* • 1909

25 Paul Klee • *Abstraction* • 1914

us back, we owe to the few — sometimes to a lone individual — who do not hesitate to go too far.

To many young painters today, Mondrian appears a model of restraint. I sense something like an echo of vague nostalgia in the notes on abstract art that Léger published in Montreal in 1945, in which he wrote:

"Of the various plastic orientations developed over the past twenty-five years, abstract art is the most important, the most interesting. It is by no means an experimental curiosity; it is an art which has value in itself, which has realized itself, and which answers a need.... Perhaps the future will classify it among *paradis artificiels,* but I do not think so. It is dominated by that same desire for perfection and for total liberation that has produced saints, heroes, and madmen. It is an extreme state which only a few creators and admirers are capable of achieving. The danger of this formula lies in the very elevation of its intentions. Modelings, contrasts, objects have disappeared, leaving only very pure, very precise relations, and a few colors, a few lines; blank spaces, without depth. Add to this a respect for the vertical plane — thin, rigid, sharp. It is a true, incorruptible purism. Robespierre would have used it to drape his goddess, Reason. It is a religion that cannot be argued about. It has its saints, its disciples, and its heretics. Modern life, with its speed and tumult, dynamic and full of contrasts, beats furiously against this light, luminous, delicate structure, which emerges coldly from the chaos. Do not touch it, it is an accomplished fact. It had to be, it is there to stay."

I like this lucid text and I cannot help thinking that at the time he wrote it Léger was somewhat behind his time (his American period is undoubtedly his least successful). In

1913/1914 with his contrasting forms he was in the very vanguard of the modern movement, together with Delaunay and Mondrian himself (whom he seems not to have known personally).

The arrival of the Futurists upon the scene was like an enormous breath of fresh air. All their revolutionary ideas radiated from their central preoccupation, spatial dynamism. There is nothing absurd in the realm of art and the Futurists, before the Dadaists, were not far from creating an art of the absurd. To try and introduce movement into painting is a hazardous undertaking, to say the least. And yet they achieved it, they made everything move. Today, when we look at the works created by Severini, Balla, and Boccioni between 1912 and 1914, we perceive that the sense-less has produced masterpieces. Once again, defiance proved to be wisdom, while the "wisdom" to which certain Futurists later dedicated themselves led to a dead end. I am thinking of Severini's disordered career, of Carrà's, and of Soffici's, an even more disappointing case. The course of art is full of such paradoxes.

But the Futurists were rarely abstract painters. They advocated political action, engaged in public debate, and sought publicity through noisy demonstrations. Such activities were hardly conducive to the cultivation of that inner vision, of that undivided attention given to the act of painting — and of the technical means of expression required by abstract painting both in its beginnings and in our own time. The Futurists' revolt against everything static was double-edged; it propelled them into admirable innovations and it created an amazing stir in the world of art. But too often they remained merely anecdotal painters: and this congenital, essentially literary failing caused the movement to culminate in the *aeropittura futurista*, which by 1930 was nothing more than wholly academic *passéiste* painting (to use the word coined by Marinetti to designate the enemies of Futurism). All that remained was the flourish — a set of declamatory gestures suitable for every occasion.

But we are still in the period before 1914, and we must pay tribute to the works being created at that time by the pioneers, whose importance has perhaps not yet been fully measured. I am thinking especially of Severini's *Dance Rhythms, Dynamic Hieroglyphic of the Bal Tabarin* (1912), and his *Dance of the Tam-Tam at the Monico* (1911), a big painting which has been lost. Here, we see crowds swept by a single rhythm, in paintings composed entirely of jagged, jolting lines, and in the brightest, most clashing colors. They are a kind of prefiguration of jazz, whose syncopated rhythms were to flood Europe only a few years later. The painter treats his themes, which are basically very simple, exactly as a jazz musician who plays a melody, distorts it, tantalizes it, loses it, and again recovers it.

In April, 1910, the *Technical Manifesto of Futurist Painting* had appeared. It was signed by Boccioni, Carrà, Russolo, Balla, and Severini, and behind it could be sensed Marinetti's poetic inspiration. "Everything moves, evolves, is transformed from moment to moment," it states. "An outline never remains static to our eyes, but is constantly appearing and disappearing. Given the persistence of the image on the retina, objects in movement multiply, become deformed, and chase one another, like hurried vibrations in the space through which they pass.... A running horse has twenty legs, not four, and their movements are triangular." This kind of writing, so typical of the first manifestos, had a powerfully liberating influence on a whole generation. When the Futurist painters declared that the viewer is no longer to be placed in front of the painting but inside it, I think they meant not only that the canvas and the viewer share the same indivisible space, but that they expected him to participate fully in the painter's work through a similarly creative enthusiasm. Actually, what would be left of art — and especially of abstract art — without this mysterious sympathy, without this "calm love" that first creates attachment, then communicates this attachment, to others, thereby giving the work a lasting power that finally passes into history.

Arriving at the point of view of pure abstraction, we perceive that the Futurists were both closer to and farther removed from it than the Cubists. This is because their field of action was much broader, and their antitraditionalism attacked everything, fed on everything. Certain of Severini's Divisionist works, although called "dancing girl" or "dance," are wholly abstract, as are also his pasted papers of the same period (*Geometric Portrait of Cravan*, 1912). Abstract, too, are such paintings as Carrà's *Centrifugal Forces* (1912), Boccioni's *Dynamism of a Human Body* (1913), and Balla's *Forms of Moods* (1914). But these "incunabulae" of abstract painting are, in a sense, accidents. The purpose of the Futurists was to plunge their art into life, into the street, and to break up everything that was stagnant, everything that was sheer habit. This will to action and this sensory participation is the indelible seal that marks all their works.

Though one would hardly guess it from the static quality of his painting and the calmness of his spirit, Piet Mondrian held the Futurists in high esteem. Marinetti, who was sensitive to the slightest sign of approval and whose capacity for enthusiasm was much more highly developed than his critical sense, had immediately decreed that Mondrian was "the greatest Futurist painter of the North."

But what Mondrian admired in Futurism was not so much its painting as its climate of liberation from the past it was trying to create in art and in life. His natural placidity did not exclude an obscure resentment against the slowness with which the world moves and against the sluggishness of certain intellectuals. The Futurists' war of movement was the strategic complement of his own war of attrition.

This unshakable position which was to be his for so many years, was being consolidated during 1912/14, the same years that the Futurists were galloping in all directions like fiends let loose, clearing an immense field before the very measured steps of the future creator of Neo-Plasticism. The Futurists had swarmed from the south (somewhat like Renaissance *condottieri*) counting on lightning tactics to take possession of Paris; Mondrian, coming from Holland, forever on the defensive against the sea, and which it has partly pushed back by dint of immense patience, was barely to make his presence known in the course of his first stay in Paris, and made hardly more of a stir when later on he lived and worked there for twenty years.

His painting underwent a profound transformation during the two and a half years of his first stay in Paris. But he was never one to resort to shortcuts: Mondrian's pace allowed neither a leap forward nor a stepping aside nor the slightest distraction. He moved surely, without letting his work get ahead of his ideas, nor the ideas get ahead of the work. But advance he did, even though it was by small steps. All his life he was to worry as to whether the last canvas was an improvement on the preceding one. He was so obsessed by the idea of going further, even further, still a little further, that he was tempted to regard as negligible, even to reject as unpardonable errors, the achievements of the previous stage. But for him, 1912 was also an eventful year. That year he painted the two versions of the *Still Life with Ginger Pot,* the *Appletree in Bloom* (Gemeentemuseum, The Hague), as well as the admirable abstract composition in curved lines with a discreet background of horizontal-vertical lines entitled *Trees in Bloom,* the gray and ochre *Composition No. 11* (Kröller-Müller Museum), various studio improvisations on the subject of the tree in which the horizontal-vertical theme appears more and more clearly, as it also does in two very fine paintings with subdued highlights entitled *Nude* and *Feminine Figure.* This simple rhythmic theme becomes more explicit in 1913, and finally crystallizes in the paintings and drawings of 1914 and 1915. In 1913 Mondrian painted the *Composition in the Oval* in gray and ochre (Stedelijk Museum in Amsterdam) the great golden canvas in the Guggenheim Museum in New York, the blue-gray canvas in the Kröller-Müller Museum, and a remarkable oval composition (Museum of Modern Art in New York) in which the very short curved strokes and three short diagonals create a harmonious balance with the horizontal and vertical lines, the whole set against a background of discreet colors in which white dominates.

In 1914, the horizontal-vertical theme became strongly accentuated in *Composition III* (Stedelijk Museum) and in numerous compositions most of which are called "Façades" and which tend toward monochrome gray. Back in Holland late the same year, Mondrian executed a great number of large drawings (sometimes incorrectly dated 1912) which are abstracts of the façade of the church of Domburg, or of trees, or of the sea at Scheveningen (the last generally entitled *The Sea* or *Pier and Ocean).* With the "scaffoldings" drawn in Paris, all these themes finally converge, in the abstract compositions of 1916 and 1917, of which the most consummate example is the black-and-white painting,

Composition with Lines, which is now in the Kröller-Müller Museum.

It should be noted that the rhythm of the short horizontal and vertical lines had been emphasized as early as 1910 in numerous works by Braque and Picasso, not least of these being Braque's delicate engravings between 1910 and 1912. Mondrian also owes the use of the oval to the example of these two Cubist masters. A remark attributed to Braque is very pertinent here: "Thanks to the oval," he is supposed to have said, "I have discovered the meaning of the horizontal and the vertical." The attraction which the oval exerted on the Cubists and on Mondrian can be easily understood: the presence of the curved line makes it possible, by opposition, to accentuate the straight lines. The closed form induces a sounding of the infinite.

But this undeniable influence of the Cubists combined in a very special way with a tendency which had long been shaping in Mondrian's mind. In one of the notebooks there is a jotting which, to judge from the accompanying drawings, must date from one of his last stays in Domburg (that is, before his first trip to Paris) in 1910 or 1911, and which suggests that it was the observation of the sea that produced the first crystallization of the horizontal-vertical theme. Beneath a very explicit drawing we read these words: "Masculine and feminine, vertical and horizontal" *(Mannel. en vrouwel., vertik. en horiz.).*

To Mondrian, then, the horizontal expanse of the limitless receptacle of the sea symbolizes femininity; masculinity is symbolized by the rows of wooden piles advancing into the sea to break its waves and to protect the dunes against erosion. By imagining the prolongation of these pilings we get an image of a forest bathing in the sea, vertical trunks cutting across the horizontal line of the waves, and also the line of the horizon itself at right angles. Such is the origin of Mondrian's theme, of the fundamental dualism which was later to become the basis of Neo-Plasticism. This aesthetic system was to rest entirely upon the dogma of the right angle, already provided, broadly speaking, by the horizon of the sea and the vertical opposition of the dunes. Thus the Scholastic dogma to the effect that nothing is in the mind which was not first in the senses, was confirmed by the least sensuous of all painters.

When we pass from Mondrian to Kandinsky we leave one world for another, even though they carried out their investigations more or less at the same time, and especially during the crucial period we are dealing with. The two men felt little attraction for each other. I was present when they met for the first time, in 1930, in the *Cercle et Carré* group, and their conversation on this occasion scarcely went beyond a few conventional courtesies. Later on, when Kandinsky came to live in Neuilly, their relations do not seem to have greatly improved. "I don't care for him," Mondrian said toward the end of his life when he was asked about Kandinsky.

Two such dissimilar forces (giants of painting) could but exclude each other. This other giant came from Russia, with the fantastic Oriental background ever present in him, and throughout his vast work its abundant colors burst out in a great and joyous tumult. While Mondrian had formed ties with the Cubists, Kandinsky had quite logically found his affinities with the Fauves. A latecomer to painting (he was over thirty when he decided to dedicate himself to it), Kandinsky's eye had been struck and stimulated by Claude Monet's *Haystacks*. However, it was the Fauve paintings he saw in Paris, in the course of a prolonged visit in 1907, that gave him his real spur. The Russian-Oriental elements in his make-up found a sudden outlet and proceeded to assert themselves with uncommon force and boldness. His first abstract watercolor (1910) is a colored sketch which can match in vivacity and daring, any *tachiste* or nonformal painting of today.

It is true that this rapid sketch remains an isolated outpost in the evolution of Kandinsky's painting. It may be observed, however, that finished paintings like the *Improvisation on Mahogany, Composition III,* and *Improvisation 10,* all of this same year of the above-mentioned watercolor, 1910, go as far in the direction of abstraction as in the figurative of the faithful interpretation of the object. We know that Kandinsky painted landscapes, recognizable as such, until 1913. But who can tell whether the large *Composition IV* (1911), or the *Improvisation* (1912) in the Guggenheim Museum, are landscapes or fantasies of the mind? Here lies the ambiguity of all frontiers, when one abandons conventions, and I confess that these subtle distinctions strike me as idle. An art critic once claimed that he could make out a man on horseback in the "first abstract water-color." But there has been so much discussion over priority in abstract art that it is hard to avoid the labyrinth of these quibbles.

As for myself, I confess to a preference for clear-cut situations, for radical, and even extreme, positions. But I also feel a secret and very strong attraction to ambiguous situations when they are natural and not feigned. I mean, for example, that hovering moment when it is no longer day and not yet night, the shades of emotion between indifference and friendship, the region lying between the plain and the mountain, the nebulous age between childhood and adolescence. If such ambiguities are so fascinating it is doubtless because they are so undefinable. That which is pure transition is all the more appealing to the mind because of its elusiveness. It is the same in the cases of Mondrian, Kandinsky, and the Cubists: abstraction and figuration have a common frontier in their work that is so tenuous that we often do not know which side we are on. It is this ambiguity that imparts a rare poetic charm to their paintings. Artists like Klee, Miro, and Dubuffet have also pitched their tents on this borderline and constantly travel from one side to the other, anxious to sow uneasiness in the observer, and, at the same time, uneasy themselves. Passersby that we are, we must grant that this is a valid conception of life.

It was in December 1911 that Kandinsky's *Über das Geistige in der Kunst (Concerning the Spiritual in Art)* was printed in Munich. This work went through two subsequent German editions in 1912, though there was not a complete English translation until 1946, and a French translation in 1949. No book has done so much for the dissemination and under- standing of the new ideas, none sets them forth more penetratingly or more fully. It is, and will remain, one of the foundation stones of twentieth-century art, a permanent basis for comparing our century with other centuries. Let us look again at a few passages.

"When form appears to be without meaning and *says nothing* (according to the consecrated phrase), this must not be taken literally. There is no form, there is nothing in the world, which says nothing. Often, it is true, the message does not reach our soul, either because it has no meaning in and for itself, or, as is more likely, because it has not been conveyed to the right place.... Every serious work rings inwardly like the calm and dignified words, 'Here I am. Love or hatred of the work blows over it and dissolves. These words ring out eternally.... There is no 'must' in art, which is ever free. Before a 'must' art vanishes, as does day before the night."

But the main theme of the book is the affirmation of inner necessity, of an inner urge *(die innere Notwendigkeit, der innere Drang),* a kind of Bergsonian *élan vital* applied to painting. The author constantly reverts to this main theme as to the central source of his thinking.

"All means are sacred when they are dictated by inner necessity. All means are reprehensible when they do not spring from the fountain of inner necessity.... The path on which we already find ourselves today, and which is the greatest good fortune of our time, is the path which leads us away from the outer appearance of things and brings us instead to the opposite goal: the goal of inner necessity ....The artist must be blind to 'recognized' and 'unrecognized' form, deaf to the teachings and desires of his time. His open eyes must be directed to his inner life and his ears must be constantly attuned to the voice of inner necessity. Then he will be able to employ all approved means and, with equal facility, all disapproved means.... Inner necessity springs from three mystical sources. They in turn arise from three mystical necessities: 1. every artist, as a creator, must express the essence of his own personality; 2. every artist, as a child of his time, must express the essence of his period; 3. every artist, as a servant of art, must express what is the general essence of art (that is, the element of pure and timeless art which is innate in all beings, peoples, and times, and which is expressed in the work of every artist, every people, and every period, and which, as the principal element of art, knows no time or space). The eyes of the spirit need penetrate only the first two elements in order to lay bare the third. Then it is seen that the 'crudely' sculptured column of an Indian temple is imbued with the same spirit as the most living 'modern' work."

Thus the spirit breathed during the period of the *Blaue Reiter* in Munich. But of all those artists who participated in that famous exhibition, Kandinsky was the only one to offer abstract works. And even in his case, as we have seen, the choice remained indeterminate: one part of his work being ambivalent until 1913, without counting numerous returns to figurative work even much later, such as *Saint George* (1917); *With the Wooden Horse* (1917); the Moscow landscapes of 1920; and *Three Mottled Figures* (1942).

In the case of some, like Kupka, for example, the passage to pure abstraction was sudden and with no return to figurative art. Some go to Damascus and are lightning-struck (or illuminated) on the way; others, responsive only to the whims of chance, follow rural paths which are like so many convolutions of their brains. Though it seems quite simple, Kupka's case has its own complexity. We find in him a kind of spontaneous generation of free forms arising independently of any Futurist, Fauve, or Cubist influence, or else spurred by all these movements at one and the same time. It is amazing to see with what ease he passes from one form to another, from the simplest to the most baroque, from the arabesque with very pure lines to Symbolist turgidity. The fact is that the painter lived for a long time in the climate of the so-called "modern style" or Art Nouveau of the 1900s, and found it hard to break away from it completely. For all his unevenness as an artist, he achieved greatness when he chose to, and in any case he remains one of the authentic pioneers of modern art.

Kupka, then, participated in the Fall Salon of 1912 with two works which created general consternation and which are undoubtedly the first paintings to propose, with no retreat, a radical renewal of Cubism. In 1913, he exhibited in the same Salon *Localizations of Graphic Mobiles I and II*, while at the Salon des Indépendants he showed *Vertical Planes* and *Brown Line Solo*. The painter seemed to take a certain pleasure in exhibiting side by side canvases which mutually negated one another, perhaps in order to emphasize thereby the caprices of inspiration. Kupka's production was in this sense capricious until his death — capricious and jolting, but never frivolous. It is perhaps the absence of humor, of the lighter side of the spirit, which has made it so difficult for his painting to "get off the ground" in Paris. Yet it is full of loftiness: *Language of the Verticals* (1911), *Blue and Red Verticals* (1913), *Philosophic Architecture* (1913), *Sonorous Verticals* (1921), *Elevations* (1938).

In the spiritual climate of Delaunay we find — and we are still in 1912 — two American painters: Morgan Russell and Stanton Macdonald-Wright. Although they got their training in Paris, and their painting is visibly influenced by Delaunay's Orphism, they refused to enlist under this banner. When they exhibited in 1913, first in Munich and then in Paris (at Bernheim-Jeune's), calling themselves "synchromists." It was by this designation that history was to adopt the first two American abstract painters. And nothing appears more justified than this distinction.

They were very young. Morgan Russell was twenty-six in 1912, and Macdonald-Wright was barely twenty-two. Encouraged by the latest novelties in painting to be seen in the great Paris exhibitions, they seem to have entered the contagious climate and fell prey to the itch of all the colors simultaneously, and nothing would do but they must at once transcribe these on canvas. The bloodless crime that they committed (premeditated it seems, for they also wrote) was a felicitous transcription of energy and frankness. The lyricism they achieved through color, exactly as in the case of Delaunay, in no way negated their sense of structure. But their art is very different from that of the French painter. Russell uses clashing geometric forms, trapezoidal by preference, with or without alternating curves. His main work is the very large *Synchromy to Form* which was shown at the Salon des Indépendants in 1914. No less remarkable is a *Synchrony in Four Parts No. 7* of 1914 (Whitney Museum in New York), a sort of disarticulated kaleidoscope the four parts of which simultaneously reinforce and jar one another. With details that are crude and even cruel, the painter obtains a whole of perfect unity. It was a brand-new style at the time when the picture was painted.

Macdonald-Wright's manner, while not lacking in force, is more elegant, and above all more allusive than his colleague's. Hence there is a more poetic climate, a delicacy which prefigures the future orientalist (Macdonald-Wright was in fact to dedicate long years of his life to the study of ancient Japanese art, and at the present time is one of its most highly reputed authorities). The *Oriental Synchromy in Blue-Green* of 1918 (Whitney Museum) is one of his most accomplished works and announces this attraction to the East in its title. Wholly abstract paintings are rare in this first period of the artist's production, but those we know are by a first-class painter, precocious in his maturity. A few of his works attain a harmony of form and color that have rarely been surpassed.

I have before me loose sheets and pages of Morgan Russell's 1912/13 sketchbook. The numerous sketches are rich in revealing the genesis of his painting. We witness a progressive splitting-up of the object, leading to a recomposition or improvisation with the fractions: the cubist process, in other words. However Russell was very quick to reach the point where he abandoned the object altogether and began to create freely with forms and colors. On one of these sketches we read the words, scribbled in pencil, "There is purposely no subject (image), it's to exalt other regions of the mind."

Another American in Paris at this time was a friend of the Delaunays and exhibited with them in the Orphist group at the Salon des Indépendants in 1914. His name was Patrick Henry Bruce. His work has been in large part destroyed. All that survives of this first period are a few paintings in the Yale University collection. These works are rather close to Morgan Russell's style — a style which Bruce was later to develop in the direction of cubed forms, sharply individuated, the third dimension being freely employed in order to create, it would seem, a new spatial density.

All three painters participated in the Armory Show of 1913. But a few years later Morgan Russell and Macdonald-Wright returned to figurative painting, the former for good (he died in 1953), the second to revert to new Synchromist themes in 1953, after several visits to Japan.

By all accounts the artistic climate in Russia during these pre-war years was extraordinary. For the exact dates of the works created during this period, however, it is less easy to find agreement. It is undeniable, in any case, that Larionov and Gontcharova exhibited at Paul Guillaume's in Paris, in June 1914. Of some forty paintings shown, approximately fifteen were altogether abstract. The show was a kind of retrospective of their Russian work, serving to introduce them to Paris, and Guillaume Apollinaire was lavish in his praises in the catalogue of the exhibition. It is only too obvious that all these paintings had not been executed during the course of the year in which they were exhibited. This fact alone, and the diversity of the works shown, serves to stress the historic importance of the two painters and the boldness of their pre-1914 explorations.

They were above all the inventors of "Rayonism" (ray-ism), a word that was perhaps coined as a reply to Cubism. Nothing is more opposed to the plasticity and weight of the cube than the flash of light. The manifesto of Rayonism, signed by Larionov, appeared in 1913. But it seems quite probable that Larionov's and Gontcharova's canvases in this style had been painted much earlier. I have had the opportunity of seeing reproductions of two Rayonist works by Larionov — works which are altogether abstract — in a publication that appeared in Moscow in 1912. In these paintings the influence of the Futurist manifestos, which had circulated widely in Russia, seems obvious. As we know, everything that was being done in Paris was known almost immediately in Moscow, thanks especially to the activity of the collectors Shchukin and Morosov who, like Diaghilev, spent their time between Moscow and Paris. In 1914 Larionov and Gontcharova, who were very close to Diaghilev, abandoned painting almost completely and devoted their talents from then on to the famous *Ballets Russes*.

A similar difficulty in the dating of works is attached to the name of Malevich. It is hard for me to believe that this painter can have lied when he wrote in his book, *The Non-Objective World* (originally published in 1927 as *Die Gegenstandlose Welt*): "During the year 1913, in my desperate attempt to free art of the useless weight of the object, I resorted to the square and exhibited a painting that represented nothing more than a black square against a white background...." The date of 1913 is repeated ten times in the same book beneath reproductions of works by Malevich, the date of 1914 twice, the date of 1914/15 once, 1915 four times, 1916 three times, etc. Whatever one may think of these specific indications or of the accuracy of these dates, the study of the documents of the period, patiently carried out by M. Habasque, brings out the fact that Malevich's Suprematist works were not exhibited before 1915, which is in fact the date of the Russian edition of this work.

This being said, we cannot fail to recognize the exceptional audacity of having presented to the public as a work of art, whether in 1915 or in 1913, a simple square drawn in graphite.

From his Fauvist, Cubist, and Cubist-Futurist antecedents, Malevich pushed on to the pure and simple plane, and from there to the spelling out of the primary elements: the circle, the cross (or two planes cutting across each other), the triangle, the straight line, and the broken stroke. It was with this alphabet that he began to write his style of painting, a kind of aerial construction, which he called "Suprematism." It was related to Constructivism, invented by Tatlin, a sculptor-painter, and also to Rodchenko's Non-Objectivism. The two last-named artists gave up original art some time after the advent of Communism in Russia and from this time on concerned themselves only with techniques of applied art. Malevich, defenseless and without means, continued the struggle in Leningrad, where he died in 1935. Many of his works are to be found in the Peggy Guggenheim collection in Venice, at the Museum of Modern Art in New York (in particular the famous *White on White* of 1919), and in greater number, at the Stedelijk Museum in Amsterdam.

A few isolated forerunners must be mentioned here. Francis Picabia had painted a canvas bearing the title *Rubber* as early as 1908 and had also turned out a number of abstract drawings. Joseph Lacasse, while still a very young man working in a stone quarry, had executed some remarkable gouaches between 1909 and 1912; they could have been the work of a Poliakoff working in *grisaille*. Baranoff-Rossiné, a bewildering painter if ever there was one — a tortured soul and an uneven artist — intermittently turned out abstract paintings. The Musée d'Art Moderne in Paris has a strange, large, untitled painting of his, dated 1910. The Austrian artist, Stolbach (as early as 1906 I am assured) executed a great number of drawings, some of which are closely related to certain investigations regarded as novel even in 1960.

I cannot fail to mention some abstract "Impressions" by Degas which were exhibited in Paris some years ago, and which are strangely close to the present-day works of our blurry nonformal painters. We know that Claude Monet is openly recognized as an ancestor and a master by a whole group of Parisian abstract painters. I know a large study by Monet, in a small local museum in the south of France — apparently one of the studies he made for the *Nymphéas* — which could easily pass for an abstract painting. What does the brand of the liquor matter, so long as one can get drunk on it! The intoxication that today's young painters derive from the *Nymphéas* (unjustly forgotten for some time) is in any case an intoxication that does not lead to extravagance.

But long before Degas and Monet, there was that other forerunner whose pre-abstract impressions — of Venice, for

26   Emilio Pettoruti • *Harmony-Movement* • 1914

example — are well known. I am referring to J. M. W. Turner. When the First World War broke out, Mondrian was visiting Holland; Klee, Pevsner, Marc, and Macke had just produced their first abstract works (the two last-named were to die at the front); Arp was in Paris — and later in Weggis, Switzerland — drawing illustrations for the *Baghavad Gita* and composing his first abstract collages (which he was later to call "Before my Birth"); Brancusi was sculpting the *Prodigal Child;* Cravan was publishing his famous Pamphlets on the Independents; Marcel Duchamp was exhibiting a rack for drying wine bottles as a work of art, thus anticipating Dadaism; in Italy, Magnelli, was painting his first large canvases with geometric forms;

Balla was painting *Mercury Passes before the Sun;* London was witnessing the birth of the Vorticist group, which owed a good deal to the Futurists and which was to give England its first abstract painter, Edward Wadsworth.

To my knowledge, no exhibition having a wholly abstract character was held before 1914. The principal public art exhibitions in which abstract works were shown (together with representational works) were the Blaue Reiter, in Munich, the Jack of Diamonds, in Moscow, the Salon des Indépendants, the Salon d'Automne, and the Salon de la Section d'Or, in Paris, the exhibits of the Modern Art Circle in Amsterdam, the Armory Show of 1913 in New York, the exhibits of the Stieglitz Gallery in the same city, and the exhibits of the Sturm Gallery in Berlin.

A mass of new material was spread out, to create the art of this century. It was possible to build (and yet the demolition instruments were also included among the building tools). But rarely, in the forty years to follow, was anyone to do better than had already been done by a few creators with limited means and utterly devoid of vanity. Rarely was anyone to do as well.

PART TWO

From 1915 to 1940

How many good things in life we owe to chance encounters! It is to the meeting of Mondrian with Theo van Doesburg at the end of 1915 that we owe the creation, two years later, of *De Stijl* ("the style"). A small group of men, a fighting little magazine, gave birth to a great movement which was to exert, and which still exerts, a telling influence on one of the main tendencies of the art of this century. Van Doesburg was an intellectual in quest of adventure — and what adventure is finer for an intellectual than a powerful idea? Mondrian was Van Doesburg's great discovery, his powerful idea.

The two men were predestined to understand and complement each other. Without leaving Holland, Van Doesburg had closely followed all the avant-garde developments in European art. He had published poems, numerous articles, and he painted. Mondrian's contribution was the atmosphere of Paris — the coolest and the hottest in the world — and his work. It was through his work that the contact was established — through an apparently secondary side of his work: the India-ink drawings, those that Alfred H. Barr, Jr. later called "plus-minus" works — a progressive development, a kind of meditation on the horizontal-vertical theme carried to the point of total distillation. The series had just reached the large drawing contained in an erased oval outline (Kröller-Müller Museum in Otterloo), which represents the peak of his development along these lines.

What was at issue? Essentially, it seems to have been the problem of on aesthetic harmonization of the relationship between man and his urban environment. Van Doesburg had already worked with architects, but his radical ideas found few echoes in their work, even in Holland where architecture at that time was, as we know, already close to functionalism. The horizontal-vertical rhythms of Mondrian's latest works, the austerity of the blacks and whites in the large drawings, could be the application of a pure type of architecture to painting. An architecture purer than had ever been dreamt of at that time. Hence the terms *plastique pure* and *nouvelle plastique* (in Dutch *zuivere beelding* and *nieuwe beelding*). His encounter with Mondrian's work, a touchstone of his own reflections, revealed to Van Doesburg the existance of an architecture of the spirit, free of contingencies — a concept that could become the basis of a system, a concept that was the kernel of *De Stijl*. For a moment Van Doesburg thought of completely eliminating the collaboration of architects in *De Stijl*, in order that its principle might remain uncompromised. He finally decided against this measure, however, and the first issue of the movement's magazine was published with the collaboration of the architects Oud, Wils, and Van 't Hoff, the painters Mondrian, Van der Leck, and Huszar, the painter-sculptor Vantongerloo, and Van Doesburg himself, a painter, architect, and, under the pseudonym of Bonset, a poet.

We can follow the progress of Mondrian's work during these years step by step. First the short stroke becomes a plane, then longer lines gradually split up the canvas into multiple planes, which progressively spread, finally culminating in the very fine duality-unity of his square paintings of 1928/1932 with few lines and planes. His work is a kind of conquest of silence, a slow exploration-in-depth of the void, a void in whose crucible Being affirms itself by utter renunciation. Mondrian's paintings are dematerialized, ascetic canvases, translating a minimum of carnal presence by means of a maximum of spiritual presence.

This development is accompanied by writings which explain the work in terms of basic ideas constantly repeated. Articles, essays, and dialogues in a Platonic style present and reiterate the philosophy of the horizontal-vertical theme, a philosophy based on notions of juxtaposition, relation, balance, and structure. One is struck by the clarity with which the ideas are defined, even in the first article that Mondrian published in *De Stijl*. I can account for clarity by the years of reflection which preceded, as well as by his abundant notations (no longer extant), but also by the intellectual support which Mondrian found in the Dutch philosopher Schoenmaekers, with whom he was in friendly contact in 1917/18, and whose works on mystical mathematics, based on Hinduism, were familiar to him. And surely he also found comfort and strength for his own ideas by reading Henri Poincaré, whose *Valeur de la Science* (1906) was highly esteemed in intellectual circles. Here is a passage which may surprise readers familiar with Mondrian's own writing (the italics are mine):

"Sensations are not transmissible, or rather, their purely qualitative properties are not transmissible. The same, however, does not apply for *relations* between sensations.
"From this point of view, everything objective is devoid of all quality; it is purely *relative*.... Consequently only *relations* between sensations can have an objective value.... It is only in these *relations* that objectivity must be sought ...it is these *relationships* alone that can be regarded as objective."

Does this not read like a fragment of an article written by Mondrian between 1917 and 1920?

Mondrian's almost Olympian calm, his search for the simplest elements, for the reduction of pictorial means, forms a sharp contrast to Van Doesburg's nervous feverishness in bringing to *De Stijl* the diverse values which his flair discovered. The brief works Van Doesburg published from 1917 to 1919 draw upon a vast fund of information combined with a rare perspicacity. This remarkable team, one contributing the ideas, the other the impetus, constituted the essential substance of the magazine, at least until Mondrian left *De Stijl* in 1924.

The principles of *De Stijl* are well known: the right angle in its vertical-horizontal position (which Mondrian called the "firm support"), and the use of the three primary colors, to the exclusion of all shading or mixing.

In his Manifesto of Elementarism of 1924, Van Doesburg proposed inclining the right angle to 45 degrees in order to obtain a more dynamic effect. Mondrian immediately disavowed this as heresy and ceased to contribute to the magazine.

At the very moment when *De Stijl* was publishing its first issue Russia was undergoing a political upheaval. The October Revolution exerted a powerful appeal on the Russian avant-garde artists, many of whom were to be given high posts in the teaching and administration of the fine arts. Kandinsky, Malevich, Chagall, Pevsner, Tatlin, and many other Constructivists, Suprematists, and Cubist-Futurists became government-officials until 1921, when the new directives of the Party launched the official doctrine of Socialist Realism, which still prevails today. Many Russian artists, and not the least gifted, thereupon left the country.

Those who submitted to the new laws were paralyzed artistically and were no longer heard from. A few, given official missions to organize exhibitions of Russian art in Paris, Berlin, and London, did not return to their homeland.

Yet there had been high hopes. Encouragement had been given to the most advanced artists, notably Kandinsky and Malevich. Exhibitions of Constructivist art were held in Leningrad and Moscow. The most memorable event of this happy phase was the open-air exhibition in 1920 in Moscow. It was given by the brothers Gabo and Pevsner, and held on the Tverskoy Boulevard and in a music kiosk which stands there. It was at this exhibition that the famous *Realist Manifesto* was launched, proclaiming the primacy of space and the suppression of the opaque mass in sculpture. Moreover, it was this event which was to transform the painter Pevsner into a sculptor.

At just about the same period a third center of geometric abstraction had come into being spontaneously in Switzerland, a center completely separated from those in Holland and Russia by closed frontiers and armies at war. I am referring to the work done by Jean Arp and Sophie Taeuber in 1915 and 1916, and also to the paper cutouts (cut with a paper trimmer) they collaborated on in 1918. Malevich had exhibited a perfect square only once, and had immediately gone on to other geometric elements. Sophie Taeuber, however, between 1916 to 1918 executed a long series of small horizontal-vertical polychromes which are so close to the principles of *De Stijl* (apart from the free use of all the colors) that I see in them one of the most striking illustrations of the similitude of synchronically parallel ideas. What is ripe bursts. No matter where, no matter what the circumstances. And we know that at this very moment of writing there are abstract painters in the Soviet Union whose work, kept secret, is close to what is being done in Paris and in New York.

Arp and Sophie Taeuber met in Zürich, 1915, at the Tanner Gallery during an exhibition in which Arp participated. As he wrote later, it was "the capital event of my life." Of Sophie Taeuber's work, which he saw a little later, he has written as follows:

"A deep and serene silence filled her structures composed of colors and surfaces. The exclusive use of horizontal and vertical rectangular planes in the work of art, the extreme simplification, exerted a decisive influence on my work. Here I found, stripped down to the limit, the essential elements of all earthly construction: the bursting, upward surge of the lines and the planes toward the sky, the verticality of pure life, and the vast equilibrium, the sheer horizontality and expansiveness of dreamlike peace. Her work was for me a symbol of a divinely built 'house' which man in his vanity has ravaged and sullied."

Around this pure kernel of abstract art, growing with it at the same time, rose the Dadaist whirlwind. Exceptional circumstances made possible an exceptional outburst of childlike joy and creative power which will remain unique and inimitable in the history of art.

Using whatever missiles came to hand, Dada hit the bull's-eye every time. The good marksman does not need to aim because he has the target in himself and he scores in just the way that the vine-grower prunes his vine, exacting though the work be, with a casual eye.

Dada indulged in every form of fun, in every prank, and even the least of these improvised "jokes" bore considerable fruit. This heritage is still fresh today, since so many young people, in various countries draw upon it unrestrainedly, afraid neither of facile imitation nor of ponderous, short-lived jests. To all appearances, Dada was also short-lived. What served to make it historic was the Dadaists' true detachment and the fact that they managed to join the incongruous with the human element. The incongruous was provided by the time (an oasis in the midst of an era of frightful butchery) and the place (the very bourgeois city of Zürich). The human elements were the creators: Arp, Ball, Eggeling, Janco, Huelsenbeck, Richter, Sophie Taeuber, and Tzara. But even before this, in America, Duchamp, Picabia and Man Ray had anticipated a sort of Dadaism, sometimes called "Proto-Dada."

Immediately after the end of the war, the Dada spirit spread all over Europe. Very much in tune with the mood of the times, it broke out in Germany (where at moments it became political), in France (where Alfred Jarry had been preparing the ground a long time before), in Belgium, and in Holland. New names joined the list of those already mentioned: Max Ernst, Raoul Haussmann, Georg Grosz, Kurt Schwitters. Nevertheless, Dada's center remained Zürich, with the famous "Dada evenings" in the Cabaret Voltaire, so often described in books, articles, and auto-biographies. But what is less well known, in my opinion, is that there were as many conceptions of Dada, as many distinct Dadaisms as there were actors in this prodigious spectacle. Personalities as varied as Picabia, Ernst, Arp, Schwitters, Duchamp are each small complete universes having style, accent, and manias which are wholly individual. If Dada was able to bring all these individualists together in the same spiritual climate it was precisely because the freedom of the spirit was the sole rule of this climate and because the Dada movement consistently shied away from any kind of intellectual mold.

Dada has no principles, since these serve no other purpose than to be trampled underfoot by the clever. Dadaists are clever in all things because they are not afraid of being clumsy. Dadaism laughs, because the world's misfortunes are stupid. For one feeds what one combats, but no weapon is long enough to reach laughter. Then, too, Dada's laughter has a very special quality. It is a creative laughter, it is the laughter that is secretly contained in every creative work, the bravado, the *eppure*. It is the laughter of the holy spirit which flits where it wills, even in the very beard of God the Father.

The main Dadaist works in the abstract realm, aside from those of Arp and Sophie Taeuber of which I have already spoken, are the series of drawings by Eggeling for his films, *Diagonal-Symphony* and *Horizontal-Vertical Mass,* Richter's drawings, Marcel Janco's polychrome reliefs, Picabia's "mechanical" portraits, and Schwitter's collages.

From the clean-cut line, Arp was soon to pass to the capricious form when he illustrated Tzara's *Cinéma Calendrier du Coeur Abstrait* (1920). This alternation of "classical" and "baroque" styles was henceforth to be a constant in his life, an image of Arp's two natures, mystical and irreverent, which humor at times was able to fuse into a subtle unity.

After Cubism is the title of a small book by Ozenfant and Jeanneret (Le Corbusier) which appeared late in 1918 and which was the manifesto of Purism. When we read it today we admire the clarity with which the problems are stated and — almost — resolved in these pages. Alas! the finest intellectual virtues seem to have been useless in assuming the difficult succession of the peak years of Cubism. Purism failed, in any case, mainly because of its too short duration

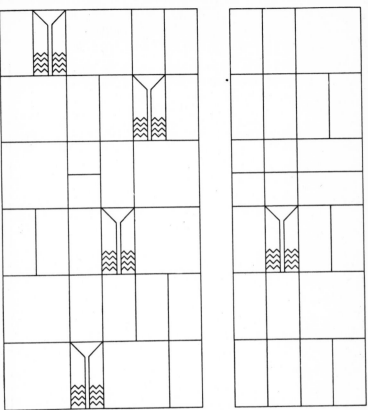

27   Sophie Taeuber-Arp • *Horizontal-Vertical Composition* • 1918

and, because of this, its too feeble development. But it is worthwhile rereading a few of the statements that appear in the pamphlet:

"The tools are at hand: with the use of raw material we must build works that will make the intellect react: it is this reaction that counts.... Science progresses only by dint of rigor. The present-day spirit is such a tendency to rigorousness, to precision, to the best use of forces and materials, to elimination of waste — in short, a tendency to purity. This is also the definition of Art. Art has also concerned itself with recreating its language, with rediscovering the means available to it; Naturalism, Impressionism, and Cubism have liberated us from bad habits and ossified traditions. Now we must build works that really belong to our time.... Enough of games. We aspire to a grave rigorousness.... We want no part of works exploiting effects that are accidental, exceptional, impressionistic, inorganic, rebellious, or picturesque. What we need are works of relevance, works that are static, works expressive of the immutable."

As we see, this is a sharply anti-Dadaist position. Thus, once again, we note the ever simultaneous presence of the two poles of the art of this century: the style and the expression, the rule and the upsurge.

As for the heritage of Cubism, I think that the Purists, far from carrying it a step — or even a yard — farther, fell short even of Cubism, precisely because they were too much concerned with stylizing the object — bottle, glass, carafe — solely as a matter of principle. The Cubists displayed a royal indifference to the object, or else, according to their humor or their whim of the moment, they treated it, with the most insolent freedom.

What was to emerge from Cubism (to borrow the subtitle of a book by Albert Gleizes) was clearly shown by the Neo-Plasticists and the Suprematists in their writings as well as in their paintings: it was pure geometry. Thus the succession claimed by the Purists had dropped from their hands even before they published their manifesto, however intelligent it may have been.

Better even, and above all more radically than the Russian movements (which were in any case to be short-lived), it was Mondrian and his co-workers of De Stijl who drew the logical conclusion from Cubism, and it was through their writings and their works that these new ideas were to spread through Europe. It is true that art is indifferent to logic — and the Cubists in disdaining their own heritage made this clear — but history, at times, takes this into account. *Guernica* may well be the (belated) masterpiece of Expressionism, Braque may well have painted magnificent studio interiors and highly sensitive landscapes; but never again would either of them achieve the level of work from their Cubist period. History, a cruel logician, was busy elsewhere.

A multitude of combative "little magazines," leading a precarious life, sprang up in every corner of Europe at about this same period. They constituted the liveliest ground of intellectual exchange during the twenties. Besides *De Stijl* in Holland, and *Der Sturm* in Berlin (both of which continued to appear and were to last until 1932), we must mention *Blok* in Warsaw, *Zenith* in Belgrade, *Ma* in Vienna, *Manomètre* in Lyon, *Merz* (edited by Schwitters) in Hanover, *The Next Call* (edited by Werkman) in Gronigen, *Het Overzicht* and *Ça ira!* in Antwerp, *Sept Arts* in Brussels, *G* (for Gestaltung) in Berlin (edited by Richter and Lissitzky),

Contimporanul and *Punkt* in Bucharest, *Pasmo* in Prague, A.B.C. in Zürich, and above all *l'Esprit Nouveau,* first edited by Paul Dermée, then by Ozenfant and Le Corbusier, followed in 1927 by the single issue of *Documents Internationaux de l'Esprit Nouveau,* edited by Dermée and myself. Finally, in 1926, *Cahiers d'Art* came into being, under the editorship of Christian Zervos. This publication is the still living ancestor of the important art reviews published today that distribute throughout the world the annals and the day-to-day events of the art of our time. However, the climate that prevailed in 1920 can in no way be compared with that of today. To begin with, there was practically no public and the little avant-garde art reviews had no other readers other than those directly interested in them. Were there at that time even ten persons in the world who bought abstract art? Disaffection was everywhere visible, a retreat seemed imminent. Many ceased to paint, some found refuge in figurative painting which, with one or two exceptions, was not to bring them the success they had expected. Those who persisted needed sound virtues of endurance, if they had no independent income. An exhibition of *De Stijl* at the Galerie de l'Effort Moderne (Léonce Rosenberg) in 1923 was surrounded by a wall of indifference. Mondrian, who had sold nothing, saw the collapse of his hope of being sponsored by the only gallery in Paris that had ever solicited him, and he was on the verge of despair. In secret he painted flowers in order to subsist. Kupka was not more favored.

The fact remains that the traces of certain unknown or forgotten painters, whose names can be found in the above-mentioned magazines of those years, often displayed prefigurations of the successful painting of today. We are surprised, for example, to see that the investigations in black

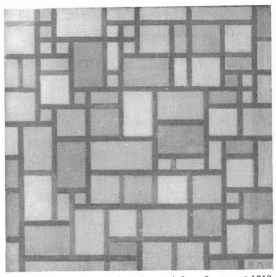

28   Piet Mondrian • *Composition in Bright Colors with Gray Contours* • 1919

29   Theo van Doesburg • *Composition* • 1919

30 Fernand Léger
Serigraph after a mural composition of 1924

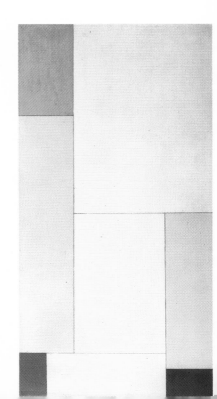

32　Antoine Pevsner • *Gray Scale* • 1920

31　Georges Vantongerloo • *Composition XV Derived from the Equation Y =
ax² + bx + 18* • 1930

33   Sophie Taeuber-Arp • *Watercolor* • 1927

34   Marcel Janco • *Bright Morning Sun* • 1918

35   Victor Servranckx • *Opus 20* • 1922

36   Wassily Kandinsky • *The Red Spot* • 1921

37   Wassily Kandinsky • *Arrow Toward the Circle* • 1930

38   Joan Miró • *Landscape* • 1930

39   Sonia Delaunay • *Catalogue cover for an exhibition in Stockholm* • 1916

40 Robert Delaunay • *Rhythm 579* • 1934

41   Piet Mondrian • *Composition with Red, Yellow, and Blue* • 1921

42   Jean Gorin • *Composition No. 9* • 1934

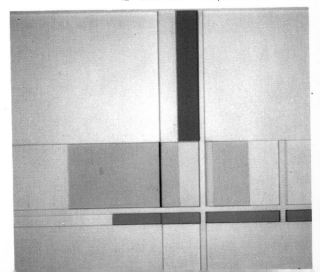

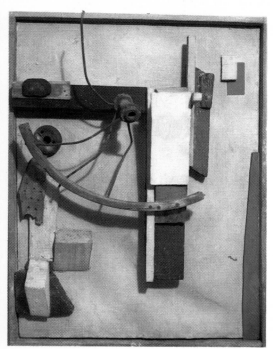

43 Kurt Schwitters • *Small Home for Seamen* • 1926

44 Auguste Herbin • *Composition* • 1939

45 Kurt Schwitters • *Merzbild* • 1922

46 Serge Charchoune • *Ornamental Cubism* • 1927

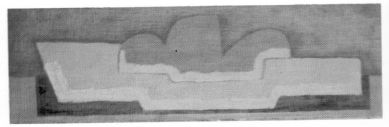

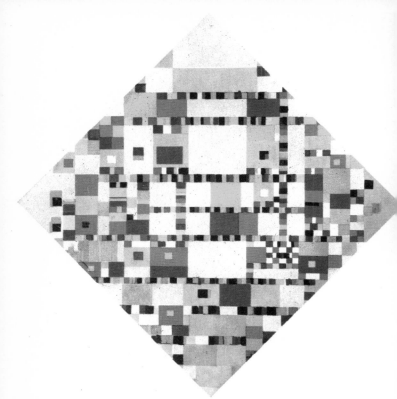

47   Piet Mondrian • *Victory Boogie Woogie* • 1944

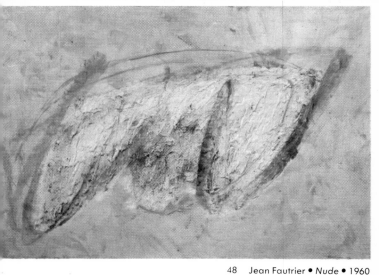

48   Jean Fautrier • *Nude* • 1960

49   Jean Atlan • *Untitled* • 1959

50 Alberto Magnelli • *Sonorous Border* • 1938

51 Nicolas de Staël • *Football Players at the Parc des Princes* • 1952

52 Geer van Velde • *Composition* • 1951

53 Bram van Velde • *Painting* • 1960

54   André Lanskoy • *Atrocities of the Reds* • 1959

and white — then very current — are at times close to the present-day achievements of Vasarely in their same play of oppositions. Which by no means diminishes the merits of the latter, whose optical investigations are far-reaching, but speaks eloquently for the minor works of the years 1920/24.

In 1922 Berlin was almost a dead city. Inflation and poverty had spread a choking blanket over it. Intellectual life had taken refuge in the avant-garde artists' and writers' clubs. And all these intellectuals would meet every evening in the homes of a few privileged individuals of the moment who gave reception after reception. Gatherings that were like the lighter joints that relieve the dreariness of dark gray wall. All races rubbed elbows in these circles; there was a lot of talk (in all languages) about abstract art, Russian politics, Buddhism, and the new architecture. To love France was the honored rule. Everything that happened in Paris found an extremely sensitive response, the most minute fact of Parisian life was immediately known, commented on, and amplified. Everyone had already forgotten the war.

Somewhere near the Kurfürstendamm, the Futurists had opened a *casa futurista* where Marinetti gave lectures. There I had a brief, somewhat sybilline discussion with the inventor of "words at liberty," but one which had a catalytic effect on the young man of twenty I was at that time. In his lecture, Marinetti had drawn a great lesson from the example of the waves of the sea, no two of which are alike and yet which ceaselessly slap against one another in a kind of endless and universal combat. I could recognize the man who had written that war is the world's only form of hygiene. When he had finished his speech, I asked the brilliant speaker if he had ever happened to look at the horizon line which remains ever the same, calm and immutable: Being and Becoming here confront each other, both enveloped in the same image. The sea horizon held a deep fascination for me ever since childhood. The Italian poet seemed to take no account of its existence and dismissed my question with some remark about "the dreams of Northerners."

Today, as then, I have the impression of witnessing the irreducible opposition of these two world views. On the one hand, there is stylist or the perfectionist who thinks in terms of concepts and tends to simplify the given. On the other hand, there is the active realist who has faith only in the empirical evidences of his own senses. This is expressed in abstract art by a certain geometry and a certain algebra.

Paradoxically, it is the dreamers who build, and who by virtue of this are finally the most realistic. Those, on the other hand, who allow themselves to be guided solely by their feelings become their own destroyers by pouring themselves out without restraint. Thus the nonformal painters turn out works which, at best, furnish material for psychiatric case histories. Case histories which in effect destroy one another as the waves of the sea collide and annul one another. A battle which unfolds beneath the narrowed eyes of the horizon. The sly horizon which is the sum of these psychological details: Mondrian and Pollock.

The creation of the Bauhaus was a considerable event in Germany, especially when Klee, Kandinsky and Moholy-Nagy, were appointed professors there in 1922. Theo van Doesburg had made a spectacular appearance at the Bauhaus the previous year, and the memory of it had not faded when I visited there in 1928. The radical and revolutionary ideas of the editor of *De Stijl* (which created turmoil in the minds of the professors) seem to have exerted an irresistible attraction on the students, who flocked to the private courses he gave in the apartment a friend had placed at his disposal. "Van Doesburg's preoccupation with the problems of pure form," says Walter Gropius, who was then the director of the Bauhaus, "did not accord with the ideal of the Institution, which was to educate the individual in the interest of the entire community." Whatever one may think of the stir caused by Van Doesburg's sojourn in Weimar (and the discussion on this subject is, even today, by no means closed), it seems that the vigor of his ideas and the fire of his eloquence also brought new insights: because this episode, violent though it may have been, was later to lead to the publication of Mondrian's *Neue Gestaltung* and Van Doesburg's *Grundbegriffe der neuen Gestaltenden Kunst* (both in the Bauhausbücher series).

Mondrian's work is a German translation of his pamphlet *Le Nèo-plasticisme, principe général de l'équivalence plastique*, first published in Paris in 1920, together with four articles, three of which had appeared in *De Stijl* between 1921 and 1923. Let us reread a few passages from these essays:

"Neo-plasticism has its roots in Cubism. It could just as easily be called the Painting of Real Abstraction, since the *abstract* can be expressed by a plastic reality.... It achieves what all painting has tried to achieve, but has been able to express only in a veiled manner. By their position and their dimension as well as by the importance given to color, the colored planes express in a plastic way only relations and not forms. Neo-Plasticism imparts to these relations an aesthetic balance and thereby expresses universal harmony.... For the moment, what art has discovered must still

55   Jozef Peeters • *Linoleum print* • 1920

be limited to art itself. Our environment cannot yet be
realized as a creation of pure harmony. Art today is at
the very point formerly occupied by religion. In its

deepest meaning religion was the transposition of the natural [to another plane]; in practice it always sought to achieve harmony between man and untransposed nature. Generally speaking, so do Theosophy and Anthroposophy, although these already possessed the original symbol of balance. And this is why they never were able to achieve equivalent relations, that is to say true harmony.

"Art, on the contrary, sought this harmony in practice [of art itself]. More and more, in its creations, it has given inwardness to that which surrounds us in nature, until, in Neo-Plasticism, nature is no longer dominant. This achievement of balance may prepare the way for the fulfillment of man and signal the end of [what we call] art."

Van Doesburg's book also abounds in general ideas. Here, taken from the last chapter, are considerations on viewing a work of art which might be read as a synthesis of Van Doesburg's and Mondrian's thinking:

"It must be emphasized that in seeing a work of art that has been composed by precise means, the viewer does not perceive dominant details. His impression is one of perfect balance to which all the parts contribute, an impression which not only applies to the parts as such, but is transmitted also to the relation existing between the work of art and the viewer. Although it is very difficult to express in words the effect of a work of art, it may be said that the viewer's deepest impression can best be defined as the achievement of a balance between objective meaning and subjective meaning, both directly penetrated by awareness. He has a sensation of height and of depth which are no longer in any way bound to natural conditions or to spatial dimensions, a sensation which places the viewer in a state of conscious harmony, the play of dominant details being no longer perceived.

"Quite possibly this aesthetic contemplation coincides with religious feeling or with the uplift of the religious spirit, since in a work of art it is the deepest inwardness that expresses itself. It is necessary, however, to bear in mind the essential distinction that the contemplation or uplift of art — i.e., the experience of pure art — contains nothing dreamy or vague. It is exactly the contrary: true artistic experience is altogether real and conscious.

"True artistic experience is never passive, for the spectator is obliged to participate, as it were, in the continuous or discontinuous variations of proportions, positions, lines, and planes. Moreover, he must see clearly how this play of repeated or non-repeated changes may give rise to a new harmony of relations which will constitute the unity of the work. Every part becomes organized into a whole with the other parts. All the parts contribute to the unity of the composition, none of them assuming a dominant place in the whole. "A perfect balance in artistic relationships is thus achieved. The viewer, with nothing to distract him, can participate in it wholly."

In the same series of the Bauhausbücher, Klee published *Pädagogishes Skizzenbuch (Book of Pedagogical Sketches)* and Kandinsky *Punkt un Linie zu Fläche (Point and Line to Plane)*. Malevich's stay at the Bauhaus in 1926/27 produced his work *Die Gegenstandslose Welt (The World Without Object)*, also published in the same series. As for the first books published by Moholy-Nagy, *Malerei, Photographie, Film* and *Von Material zur Architektur (The New Vision: From Material to Architecture)*, they abundantly reflect what was to be his major preoccupation for so many years: the search for new materials, and through them, access to unexplored, often very refreshing, possibilities of plastic expression.

The atmosphere that characterized the Bauhaus has often been described to me by both students and former professors. Without a framework devoid of rigidity, but a framework none the less, a gentle anarchy prevailed. A tragile harmony between discipline and play, between the spirit of creation and the natural inclination toward recreation. A climate particularly propitious to that rare and beneficent success which the Bauhaus was able to achieve in its finest years: the exalting friendship between students and professors.

The influence of the ideas of the *De Stijl* group very soon penetrated Flemish Belgium where, as early as 1920, Peeters, Servranckx, Maes, Van Dooren, and a few others executed works having pure geometric forms without, however, adopting the restrictive horizontal-vertical rule of Neo-Plasticism.

It was chiefly in the Flemish review *Het Overzicht,* which appeared from 1921 to 1925, that these artists manifested themselves. They were spearheaded by Peeters, who became co-director of the review at the end of 1922. This painter published several theoretical articles advocating a "community art," a close relative of the collectivist ideas often expressed by the editors of *De Stijl.* In an article published in 1923 Peeters gave this colorful advice:

"In front of a work of 'constructed' art never say: I can make nothing of it. It is not your intellect that is being appealed to, but your sensibility. This is true whether you feel it or not. If, however, you want to treat yourself to the luxury of understanding it as well, you had better be more demanding of your intellect.

"Don't ask: what does it mean? A work of art is not a piece of wizardry. A painting cannot speak.

"Don't visit exhibits and painters' studios 'to try to get to the bottom of what it is all about.' Instead, you should live with a few works of 'constructed' art around you without giving them forced attention. They will come to you when you are relaxed.

"Should a work of art be made to order for you? What right have you to complain when it does not live up to your expectations? You would do better to surround yourself with your own paintings, but don't ask artists to represent your ideas, which are not even clear to yourself. Artists create by virtue of an inner impulse and offer you the result in a spirit of love."

In Germany Kandinsky, after his return from Russia in 1921, quickly repudiated lyrical gushing and turned to geometrical invention. Alfred H. Barr, Jr. attributes this change to Malevich's influence rather than to an inner evolution, *sui generis,* of Kandinsky's work. However, Kandinsky, seems hardly to have felt any personal sympathy for his Russian colleague. Nonetheless, while certain forms dear to Malevich can indeed by found scattered through Kandinsky's work of the years 1922/24, the creative richness

they manifest is such that these works remain in a sense no less gushing and cannot be compared with the sober forms and restricted palette that we observe in the Suprematist works.

It is much more probable that Kandinsky was influenced by Klee, with whom he had close ties. Klee's poetics and cosmology are very clearly reflected in many of Kandinsky's works of the Bauhaus period.

On his return to Paris after a long stay in Portugal, Delaunay painted figurative works with few exceptions (such as the *Propeller*), and was to return to the paths of pure abstraction only after 1930 in a style closely resembling his swirling rhythms of 1912, but much more cerebral. Sonia Delaunay, for her part, was completely absorbed in the creation of multicolored fabrics for scarves, blouses, and dresses.

It was at about this same period that Domela and Vordemberge-Gildewart began their careers, and that Otto Freundlich, who had for a long time worked in a style of flat tints without still-life deception nor attempt at distinctive treatment, completely abandoned figuration. On the other hand, Macdonald-Wright and Morgan Russell, back in America after their brilliant beginnings in Munich and Paris, fell into all the traps of narrative painting which they had so courageously condemned.

The period of the mid-twenties was not, as we see, favorable to the expansion of abstract painting. Nevertheless, in this black hole in which the artists struggled, there was one bright spot. It was the show "Art d'Aujourd'hui" which the Polish painter Poznanski organized at the end of 1925 at the Syndicat des Antiquaires in Paris. Being absent from Paris, I did not visit this exhibition (I was then at Georges Vantongerloo's, in Menton), but I was told about the stir it made in the studios and the fresh hope it gave the avant-garde artists. The catalogue mentions 241 paintings by eighty-seven artists. I single out the names of Arp, Baumeister, Brancusi, Bruce, Marcelle Cahn, Robert and Sonia Delaunay, Van Doesburg, Domela, Gontcharova, Gris, Vilmos Huszar, Janco, Klee, Larionov, Léger, Marcoussis, Miró, Moholy-Nagy, Mondrian, Nicholson, Ozenfant, Picasso, Prampolini, Alfred Reth, Servranckx, Josef Sima, Valmier, Vantongerloo, Villon, Vordemberge-Gildewart. I regretfully pass over the names of several abstract painters who have left no trace.

The anonymously written preface to the catalogue deserves to be quoted in its entirety. The thought is simple, the writing clear. The reader may judge for himself:

"What is the purpose of this exhibition?

"Not to show examples of every tendency in contemporary painting, but to take stock, as completely as circumstances permit, of what is going on in *non-imitative plastic art*, the possibility of which was first conceived of by the Cubist movement.

"History shows that new forms of art have always been found absurd at first and then condemned out of hand by the public at large. A day comes, however, when people's eyes are opened, and a few of the works at least inspire a well-nigh religious awe.

"The schools represented here are no exception to the rule. All the less so because their novelty of appearance is due to the more or less complete lack of any effort to imitate things seen, to tell 'a story.'

"Traditional aesthetics has accustomed the viewer to look first for the subject, for the scenario of the work in front of him. Increasingly since 1911 painters have been eliminating the subject so as to liberate their lyricism from the fetters of reality. Musicians no longer feel bound to imitate the sounds of nature, but instead arrange sounds inherent in music itself. The type of painting shown here does not conceive of the picture as an intermediate point between nature and the viewer. Rather it attempts to act directly upon sensibility — and thereby on our minds by virtue of forms and colors alone. Photography, on the other hand, is such an intermediary; so is the older type of painting. However, a Bach fugue is not — though the nightingale's song which Beethoven imitated in the *Pastoral Symphony* is. The paintings shown here are rarely conceived of as interpretations, but more often as arrangements whose effect derives from their internal organization.

"What is the purpose of this new technique?
"To relieve art of the weight of reality, which is essentially anti-lyrical. Mankind needs an escape from reality.
"These artists share Poussin's conception of painting's ultimate objective: to give *délectation*. Their paintings are akin to modern poems — though their language is one of forms and color — whose sole aim, like that of modern music, is the expression of lyricism, the realization of the dream.
"Music means nothing to those who are deaf. Nor can the man who is not deaf make much of a piece of music if he listens to it thinking of something else, or having decided in advance not so enjoy it. To look at one of the paintings shown here and to burst out laughing, or to look for something which is not in the picture, is simply to be blind. The viewer should ap-

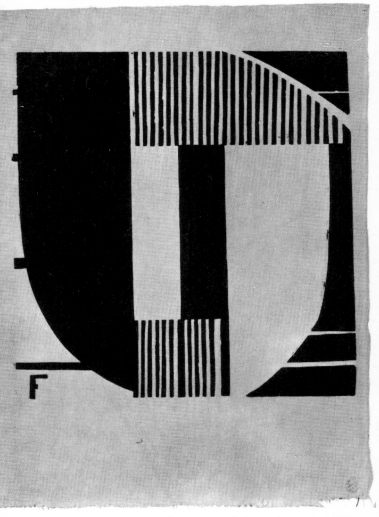

57   Otto Freundlich • *Linoleum print* • 1937

proach this painting with his eyes, with a kind of internal stillness — putting himself in a receptive, acritical mood. This attitude is necessary if the play of colored forms is to be effective, if it is to provoke in the viewer the lyrical mood which is its sole aim. Judging the work comes later.

"These pathfinders in the art of painting ask only this of you in presenting their works. Is it too much to ask?

"They are asking no more than poets or musicians do when they ask you to keep still."

The anecdote (literature, in short) was nevertheless to take possession of painting again, to dominate it as it has rarely done, when Surrealism swept over Paris. For a few years nothing was to remain of what the theoreticians and the pioneers of abstract art (they are often the same) had called "inwardness," except a bubble. A bubble which rises precariously and incongruously in the air that will presently absorb it and forget it — for the greater good of the real business of the world which is bluff, ballyhoo, high-pressure salesmanship.

Yet, in that so of-the-earth-earthy and super-real realm I perceive a somewhat bewildered maverick from these learned Freudian sessions. I am referring to Jean Arp. He brought to Surrealism his particular atmosphere in which Dada blends with metaphysics, in which navel conjugates with cloud, and in which a comma becomes both poem and constellation. In Brussels at this time he was making a series of clocks that marked a timeless time. With Sophie Taeuber, who had become his wife, he and Van Doesburg went to Strasbourg to execute the interior decorating of a café known as the Aubette. It was a big undertaking in which the genius of the three artists battled with the walls of the numerous rooms of this building without suffering injury — and for the greater good of those unhappy walls, now widowed of these works. The impious act of a philistine has torn out that fine page of the history of the art of this century. At the Aubette, Sophie Taeuber executed reliefs of a simple, clear rhythm, in the purest Neo-Plastic tradition; Arp drew great forms with ample, flowing lines, which were perhaps figures, hair, or gestures, or lamentations. Van Doesburg accomplished his finest works here: a dynamic room entirely in diagonals, and another static room in horizontal and vertical plane-reliefs. Of all these there remain only photographic reminiscences.

Around the year 1924 Miró abandoned the realistic style in which he had been painting, characterized by lines and outlined forms, and began to turn out paintings that represented nothing more than the painter's free fancy. Are they abstract? In any case, they invent a world — a new plastic world, first of all, with an unknown space. Here everything surprises: outlandishness, irony, futility, laughter, mischievousness, playfulness. Insolence is combined with delicacy, extreme purity with rank impurity. For a few years Miró brought an extraordinary freshness to modern art. Subsequently his painting became very labored, though at the same time more forceful. But he was never to recapture the childish freshness of these years when he turned out paintings that were effortlessly naïve, unquestionably abstract, and eminently poetic.

Max Ernst at this period haunted the same realms of the spirit with paintings done in broad lines, works often approaching that boundary-line where the transposition of nature and abstract composition touch. Sometimes he has reverted to this style, never dwelling on it for any length of time, a flighty demon always calling him elsewhere and waylaying him in a maze of complications. For the Surrealists, according to André Breton's dictate, were to paint dreams. But dreams, unfortunately, whether they be Freudian or otherwise, are lies of the senses, and therefore naturalistic. Hence the painting that they inspired, with debauches of talent, could only be a lie, but a studied lie. For when one claims to be dreaming while wide awake one must practice deceit, which is in itself a whole science: the science of false spiritualists. This adroit taking apart of naturalism to which the Surrealist painters committed themselves was soon to be drowned in the technique of the detail and in a rank growth of mysteries.

In March 1927, Paul Dermée and I inaugurated the literary evenings called the "Sacre du Printemps." This was the name of a small art gallery located at 5, rue du Cherche-Midi (now a flower shop). Here came Marinetti, Walden, Kassak, and Schwitters, among others; here poems were recited in all languages, sometimes to the accompaniment of a barrel-organ. Every Saturday a lively young Montparnasse crowd gathered, in greater number than the small premises could accommodate. People clustered around the doorway and in front of the windows to hear the recitations. On June 9 we received notice from the gallery's director, Jean Sliwinsky, to the effect that we had become undesirable and would have to leave. During the night someone had painted across the front of the shop *Merde pour l'esprit nouveau, tas d'idiots!* ("To hell with the new spirit! You bunch of idiots.")

We had organized a series of exhibitions of works which were all abstract. Our greatest claim to fame remains the fact that we exhibited some twenty large plates by H. N. Werkman, a Dutch printer from Groningen. He had used his printing equipment to turn out black-and-white and multicolored compositions which breathed life into the shop's usual stiff blocks and standard forms. This Werkman was a remarkable man. In his distant town he published the little review, *The Next Call*, one of the most curious magazines of the period and perhaps the only one which successfully wedded pure form and poetry. He did not need to travel to be a pure avant-garde enthusiast and to distribute to the four corners of the world more germs of novelty — and of freedom — than the great magazines of arts and letters published in Paris and London. He died as he had lived: during the German occupation of his country in World War II, grappling with a thousand difficulties, he continued to publish pamphlets exalting the freedom of the spirit in its most varied forms. This is why the Nazis shot him, obviously not knowing what they were doing and having no idea what they were doing, except that this was what they were there for. It happened on the very day Groningen was liberated.

The *Cercle et Carré* group owes its existence to my encounter with the Uruguayan painter Torrès-Garcia at an exhibition by Vordemberge-Gildewart in January, 1929. A deep friendship punctuated by quarrels united us for two years. He lived at the extreme northern end of Paris, and I lived at the opposite, southern end; he would come to my place on Sundays, and I went to see him once or twice during the week. But his need to communicate was such that he wrote me nearly every day. I still have a small volume of his letters full of ideas, thrown onto the paper pell-mell, taking issue with mine. He would get angry because I did not always answer them, or else did not write at such great length. He was a man of complete integrity, totally sincere, but of variable moods, combining great warmth with a pathological touchiness. He was a hidalgo with Indian blood.

However difficult our relationship, his obstinacy matching my patience, this unholy team of fire and water was bound to produce something. Toward the end of the year, after consulting sundry artists, including Arp, Mondrian, and Van Doesburg, we drew up the program for a new group and launched a magazine which was to be called *Cercle et Carré (Circle and Square)*.

To me, the circle and the square were the sky and the earth as symbolized by the ancient Oriental religions; they formed a kind of rudimentary alphabet by means of which everything could be expressed with the most limited means. They evoked prehistoric runes and the early Chinese *I-Ching,* or *Book of Changes.* What would come of our venture? Torrès Garcia's enthusiasm was contagious, but I was highly sceptical. Although still young (I was not yet thirty), I was weary of the perpetual Montparnasse carnival — the café reputations, the attitudinizing, the endless speeches about art — and I had a sneaking feeling that our undertaking was no longer in season. Life was something more than this, and it seemed to me that real life was to be found elsewhere. However, our meetings, which we held first at the Café Voltaire, and later at the Brasserie Lipp, were lively ones. Twenty to thirty painters attended regularly, and the eighty members cheerfully paid the monthly dues. These enabled us to bring out the first number of the magazine in March 1930 and to organize an exhibition the following month.

This exhibition was held at an art gallery which has now disappeared, at 23, rue de La Boétie, on the ground floor of the very building where Picasso lived. He was our most faithful visitor. He would come down in the morning when the gallery opened, and would sometimes remain for a long time, alone, looking in silence at one or another of the 130 works. The second number of the magazine served as a catalogue to the show, with an article by Mondrian to cap it: *L'Art réaliste et l'art super-réaliste (la Morphoplastique et la Néo-plastique)*. Among other artists represented were Arp, Baumeister, Buchheister, Marcelle Cahn, Serge Charchoune, Jean Gorin, Huszar, Kandinsky, Le Corbusier, Léger, Mondrian, Ozenfant, Pevsner, Prampolini, Russolo, Schwitters, Stazewski, Stella, Sophie Taeuber, Torrès-Garcia, Vordemberge-Gildewart, Otto van Reis, Vantongerloo, and Werkman. Also participating, though not in the catalogue, were: Freundlich, Xcéron, Moholy-Nagy, Hans Richter, and Raoul Haussmann. It was, in short, a successful coming-together. So successful that the need was felt to carry on the good work when I was taken out of circulation because of illness. Vantongerloo and Herbin took over, founding the *Abstraction-Création* group with the not yet scattered elements of *Cercle et Carré* as a nucleus.

When the review ceased to appear, it left an undeniable void. The first three numbers had had an altogether unexpected sale in the Montparnasse bookshops and elsewhere. I remember the warm encouragement I received from Robert Delaunay upon the appearance of the second issue. He returned to abstraction a few months later, and it may be that the interest aroused by *Cercle et Carré*, and a kind of breath of renovation which accompanied it, were not wholly unrelated to this.

When I came back to Paris in 1931, after a long convalescence in the south, the *Abstraction-Création* group had just been founded. Vantongerloo had been given our mailing list. At the same time I learned of Van Doesburg's death in Davos. The first issue of *Abstraction-Création* came off the press just a year later, printed in the same small dusty shop that had brought out *Cercle et Carré* and where I had earned a meager living as a non-union proofreader and make-up man. I hope I may be forgiven for recording these trivial details: are not the palpable traces of life a proof of history and the bases, however fragile, of theories?

Abstraction-Création had a much wider influence than its predecessor. From 1932 to 1936 an annual *cahier* presented reproductions and statements by painters. Beginning in December 1933, and for about a year thereafter, paintings by a few members of the group were permanently exhibited in premises looking out on a back courtyard off the Avenue de Wagram. Among the exhibitors we find the familiar names of Freundlich, Gorin, Vantongerloo, Van Doesburg, and Moholy-Nagy, but there were also new names which were later to become important: Ben Nicholson, Calder, Herbin, Paalen, Bill, Reth, and Valmier.

Issue No. 4 of *Abstraction-Création*, which appeared in 1935, gave a statistical breakdown of the group's membership. We find that there were 209 registered members in Paris and 207 throughout the rest of the world. The last figure breaks down as follows: 43 members in France (outside of Paris), 33 in America, 68 in Switzerland, 12 in Holland, 50 in the other countries of Europe, and one lone member in Japan. It seems that South America and Central America were totally absent, at this period, from the abstract realm. In 1936, when the last issue of *Abstraction-Création* appeared, Europe was in a deep slump. Hitlerism was rampant in Germany, and many artists had already fled

58   Wols • *Drawing* • c. 1947

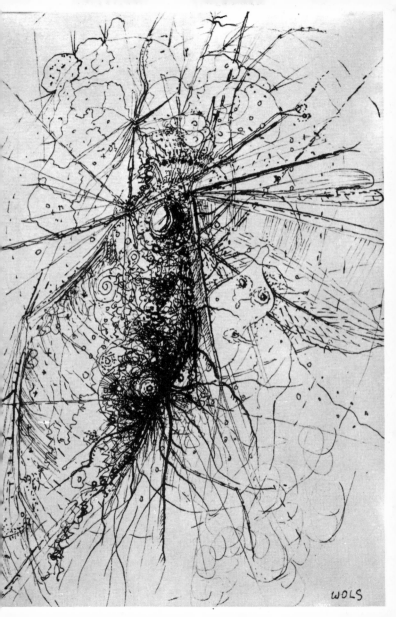

there. Italy had lined up with the Third Reich. Civil war broke out in Spain. France, villified by the dictators, appeared humiliated. There were evil portents on the horizon; night was about to descend over Europe.

It was at this moment that America took up the cause of abstract art. The Association of American Abstract Artists was founded that year, and it was also in 1936 that the exhibition *Cubism and Abstract Art* was held at the Museum of Modern Art in New York, accompanied by the important monograph by Alfred H. Barr, Jr. that bears the same title. As a matter of fact, A. E. Gallatin, with his *Museum of Living Art*, Katherine Dreier with the Société Anonyme (sponsored by Marcel Duchamp and Man Ray), and Hilla Rebay's Museum of Non-Objective Painting (now the Solomon R. Guggenheim Museum), had blazed the trail long before. These different groups continued to play an important role by educating the public, particularly the Société Anonyme with its traveling exhibitions which toured the regional museums of the United States and had familiarized Americans with the work of the pioneers of abstract art. The building up, the swift multiplication and the frequently bold orientation of the American private collections are certainly due in large part to these courageous undertakings. Nevertheless, 1936 remains a landmark in the annals of abstract art largely because of the publication of Barr's book, the first to deal with the phenomenon from a historical and methodical point of view.

At about this time a flood of refugees — artists, intellectuals, and men of science, of every origin and including the most remarkable — began to pour into the United States. War broke out in Europe, and for five years the Continent was plunged in darkness. This peaceful invasion of America, like a nervous and anguished tide, was to leave in the soil natural riches whose fruits would become visible only years later in the sudden and prodigious upsurge of American painting.

Mondrian, feeling that Paris was too vulnerable, sought asylum in London in 1939. His most perfect paintings had been produced from 1928 to 1932 — the term 'perfect' being understood in the sense of his Neo-Plastic development. These are works of small dimensions, generally square, with lines intersecting at right angles. Their studied dissymmetry and their color distribution is such that the sign is virtually canceled out. As Europe moved closer to war, and ideas of violence gained headway, the black lines multiplied in both directions as though — unconsciously? — to evoke the bars of a prison.

In London, Mondrian's canvases brightened again. But most of the paintings he began there were finished in New York. He arrived there in the early fall of 1940. The bars now became colored (as in the canvas entitled New York City, 1942), rang out (Broadway Boogie Woogie, 1942/43), and flew into splinters in a final blaze in Victory Boogie Woogie, his last work. An unfinished wonder in a lifetime of work which for thirty years had strained toward an impossible perfection with unequalled force and a tenacity.

His message was best understood in America, thanks in large part to the lucidity of Katherine Dreier, who had been a defender of Mondrian since 1926. It is only fair, therefore, that America should have become the principal heir to his work.

When this new war broke out, Schwitters had been living in Norway for a long time. There he again dedicated himself to the building of the *Merzbau* which he had had to abandon in Hanover. This fantastic tower which he had patiently erected inside his house, piercing through its three floors, was left to the mercy of the swine. The Nazi invasion of Norway had forced him to flee a second time. He took refuge in England, in Ambleside, and began his *Merzbau* all over again.

The Bible tells us that when you are persecuted in one country you must leave and find another. But do not neglect to take with you all your belongings — your art, your passion to build, to rebuild ever anew that other world in this world; that world belonging to you and which is nowhere, but in which all who are born free spirits feel at home.

For if art, like religion, belongs to no country, it is perhaps itself the only country and the only true religion. Only those hear its call who have that siren's song within them. The inner riches of the eyes bring out the secret virtues of the work, and little by little they begin to speak: they confide in those who give them their trust; they ally themselves with those who surrender something of themselves. This is what we may call enjoyment, this is what we may call possession. And these are simply other ways of saying that the sympathetic observer is in truth the co-creator of the work.

Every artist, every work of every artist, establishes, in his or its own absolutely inaccessible way, this contact of the spirit with the spirit. Provided, of course, that the viewer is in "a state of grace." A state which depends absolutely on him (receptivity is an art in itself, shutting out the world is an art in itself) and which does not depend absolutely on him, circumstances being what they are.

And let it not be said that the eyes of the beholder put more into the work than the artist himself has been capable of putting into it. One never gives too much to a work of art. It is in itself but a pretext, in the last analysis, for us to receive from ourselves what was already in us. But who does not see that the work goes beyond the one who created it? It marches before him and he will never again be able to catch up with it, it soon leaves his orbit, it will soon belong to another, since he, more quickly than his work, changes and becomes deformed, since before his work dies, he dies.

PART THREE

After 1940

Victory Boogie-Woogie, though left unfinished when Mondrian was buried in Brooklyn in February 1944, seems to open the gates to a new universe. Youth and joy are superimposed upon the gravity of the Neo-Plastic order. It is a painter's Ninth Symphony: an ending and a beginning.

Many things must disappear. The death of Freundlich in a concentration camp — a peace-loving man if ever there was one — is a symbol of this cruelty of history. When the war ended, other names would be missing from the first ranks of abstract art: Robert Delaunay, Sophie Taeuber, Kandinsky, and Mondrian himself would have ceased combat. At the same time, young germs had burgeoned in secret and would suddenly burst forth with the return of freedom.

For the moment, the center of the world was still New York, where so many generous energies had found refuge: artists, especially, were there in great number. This one may judge by those who visited Mondrian in his last illness or attended his funeral: Léger, Chagall, Lipchitz, Moholy-Nagy, Ozenfant, Hans Richter, Matta, Max Ernst, Marcel Duchamp, Xcéron, Archipenko, Glarner, Calder, Gabo, Kiesler, and a few others of lesser renown. Thanks to the presence of the avant-garde European artists, the art events that occurred in New York during the war were as exciting as those of Paris in its best years. By way of proof, one need only pick up books like *Art of this Century,* published in 1942 by Peggy Guggenheim whose fabulous collection is now in Venice, and the catalogue of the exhibition "Masters of Abstract Art" held at Helena Rubinstein's New Art Center.

The first of these contains important texts by Breton, Arp, Mondrian, Ernst, and Nicholson. The second contains Mondrian's essay, "Pure Plastic Art," followed by texts by Léger, George L. K. Morris, Stuart Davis, Hans Richter, Carl Holty, and Harry Holtzman. An unsigned introductory note shows Mondrian's influence in places. It may be of interest to look at it today:

"Abstract art does not appeal to the comparative of the conscious intellect, but to the superlative of the subconscious emotions; it is the projected intuitive expression of fundamental experience; its form is the embodiment of the artist's intuition of life, freed from the reiteration of concrete appearance.... Beneath the differences of individual *surface* are the universals of basic form — the factor which governs the relationships of part to part, of part to whole, and of the whole form to the universal environment of which it forms a part.

"Any person living in the twentieth century should know by now that physical perfection is an illusion, that quantitative or scientific knowledge is merely information or an absolute of perpetual incompletion, and that aesthetics is as near to completion or perfection as we can come, being the only qualitative form of knowledge which we possess.

"Aesthetic pleasure is the philosophical reflection of truth, and is our joy in this assurance of a universe harmonious beyond the power of accident, united in rhythm which finds echo in our own minds and feelings."

The impact of Mondrian's posthumous *Victory Boogie Woogie* soon had repercussions in Europe. Retrospective exhibitions of his work were held in Amsterdam (1946) and in Basel (1947). Paris, however, remained indifferent to the Dutch artist, even though he had lived there from 1911 to 1914 and from 1919 to 1938 and had painted a certain number of his canvases there which were already recognized everywhere else as masterpieces of the art of this century. It is worth mentioning that an obscure hostility to Mondrian's work manifested itself even in Parisian abstract art circles. A critic, very influential at the time but now forgotten, went so far as to threaten to boycott a large Paris gallery which was toying with the idea — mad though it seemed — of presenting to the Parisian public a summary of the great Mondrian retrospective that had just been held in the museums of Amsterdam and Basel. And the gallery actually did obey the critic's injunction.

Mondrian had his small revenge two years later when the Galerie Maeght, with my collaboration, organized the exhibition called "Earliest Masters of Abstract Art." The exhibition was divided into "Preliminary Investigations" and "Flowering of Abstract Art." Canvases by Mondrian were shown in both series and made a strong impression on many artists. The critics, however, ignored Mondrian entirely.

It was not until 1957 — thirteen years after the painter's death, and after the Hague, Zurich, London, Rome, Venice, and Milan exhibitions — that Paris finally saw a real Mondrian exhibition. The ever-reticent Musée d'Art Moderne having failed to come through, the Galerie Denise René offered its premises, and for this occasion published a portfolio of silk screen plates of well-chosen works, carefully reproduced.

If the situation in Paris was unfavorable to Mondrian, it was because the entrenched critics meant to concentrate all their attention to the work of Delaunay (who had died in 1941) and, even more, to that of Kandinsky (who had died in December 1944). As for living artists, the Paris critics were particularly to decide who was to be Kandinsky's "successor." Magnelli appeared to them to be the right man. I consider that a disservice was done him by calling him "Kandinsky's brilliant disciple." For there are no "brilliant disciples," and Magnelli's work can stand on its own merits. The two painters are as remote from each other, physically and morally, as Saint Basil's church in Moscow is from the Baptistry in Florence. Where Kandinsky's emphasis was always on invention, Magnelli's is on construction. For the former, painting had to be rich, varied, full of surprises, sometimes droll. It still harks back to the Nizhni-Novgorod fair under the tzars. And Kandinsky has about him something of the fair's sleight-of-hand artist who miraculously pulls objects out of his hat. One cannot help thinking of an Eastern bazaar, and there is more than a little of the fantastic element of the *Arabian Nights* in Kandinsky's art.

Magnelli is not at all a painter of this school. While he is quite disposed to indulge in play, it is always in a measured way. He betrays no flashiness, no straining for effect: we see in him the whole gravity of pre-Renaissance Italy, so aptly expressed in the compact form of the Baptistry of Florence, near which he was born. His is a highly balanced art in which the sometimes heavy grace of the forms is effectively lightened by the caprice of lines which readily change color, thus introducing a lyrical note into the monumental order.

A remarkable exhibition of large canvases by Magnelli was held in the very fine Galerie Drouin, on the Place Vendôme. This gallery played an important role in these postwar years despite the briefness of its existence. Here, in particular, were seen the first great shows of Wols, Dubuffet, and Fautrier, as well as impressive retrospectives of Picabia and Kandinsky. Other galleries were to open almost at the same time, whose mission in respect to abstract art was to be similar to that assumed by Kahnweiler for Cubism before 1914.

These were the Maeght, the Carré, and the Denise René Galleries in Paris, and the Sidney Janis and the Pinacotheca (later called the Rose Fried) galleries in New York. The proliferation of abstract art, and to a certain extent its popularization, owe a good deal to the activity and to the daring of these various galleries. Thus the Sidney Janis Gallery brought together very effective groupings of works by Mondrian, Arp, Pollock, De Kooning, Albers, the Dadaists, and the artists of *De Stijl*. The Pinacotheca presented the first shows of collected works by Schwitters, Lissitsky, Glarner, Diller, the Duchamps, and the American Synchromists. In Paris, the Maeght and Carré galleries have been active in making several young painters known, among whom may be mentioned Atlan, Bazaine, Ubac, the brothers Van Velde, Palazuelo, Arnal, Néjad, Poliakoff, and Lanskoy. It was thanks to the Galerie Carré, too, that Jacques Villon and Kupka were rescued from oblivion. As for the Galerie Denise René, it has from the beginning tended to favor Constructivist artists such as Vasarely, Herbin, Dewasne, Dayrolle, and Mortensen. Here too was held Poliakoff's first exhibition. The same gallery has also exhibited Piaubert, Reth, E. Pillet, and Le Corbusier, as well as Magnelli, Arp, Sophie Taeuber, Sonia Delaunay and a number of Constructivist painters from other European countries.

In November 1948, irritated by the confusion prevailing in

the minds of art critics regarding the origins of abstract art, Monsieur Aimé Maeght, suggested to me that I write a book in a wholly independent spirit attempting to clarify the matter under dispute. He gave me three minutes to make up my mind and three whole months to write the book. My *L'Art Abstrait, ses origines, ses premiers maîtres* thus came off the press in time for the *vernissage* of the exhibition in two parts referred to above (April 1949).

Overnight, after having been the object of a great deal of solicitude, I became the target for all attacks. I had felt called upon to correct certain biographies in order to rectify the artists' poor memories, and I was therefore called a "falsifier." I was publicly insulted. Calumny operates so insidiously that a certain artist, whose friendship I had thought to be unshakable, refused to shake hands with me for five years until finally he recognized his error. Today nothing remains of all this save a few unpleasant memories. The battle is over, the book remains. The present work is, in a certain sense, its free paraphrase and its prolongation.

De Staël and Wols were the two rising stars of the period around 1948/49. Both had experienced hard times. Both were socially refractory, though in quite different ways. De Staël lashed out at everyone, especially at his painter colleagues, and set himself a very high goal. "Braque, Matisse, and Cézanne," he said to me one day, "and nobody else — nobody."

With such an attitude, he would never "discover" America. It was America that discovered him. By the end of 1950, De Staël's paintings were to be found in and around New York in only a few private collections whose owners were greatly astonished that a writer from Paris should be able to recognize at a distance a De Staël among Picassos, Chagalls, and Juan Grises. They thought themselves to be the only ones who knew — through what secret agent? — about the painter's existence.

De Staël was a very tall, thin young man, sharp as an arrow. The scant esteem he professed for other painters made me avoid his studio. One day, at the entrance to the Musée d'Art Moderne, I had a more relaxed conversation than usual with him and I promised myself to see him again soon. He appeared to me to be more lighthearted, almost gay. A few weeks later I read in the papers of his suicide in Antibes. Paradoxical being that he was, in his last works — in which he had reverted to the figurative — he completely repudiated the bright colors of the preceding years. A transparent sadness hovered over the still lifes and the seascapes.

Wols' unsociability was a form of indolence. But he was endowed with, abundantly steeped in, the miseries of philosophy and the pit of mysticism. He let himself slump into them and painting was the drip and splash from his painful scramble back. Even Wols' tiniest works have the imprint, like Veronica's veil, of a man who daily had his fill of abysses and maelstroms. The life of his work was really to begin only after his death in 1951.

The importance accorded to Wols today appears to me at times exaggerated. Essentially his drawings and paintings, finely allusive and at times anecdotal, derive both from Surrealism and Paul Klee — lighter than the first, heavier than the second. Burrowing as they do into the recesses of a tortured spirit, they visibly tend, toward the same lyrical liberation that Kandinsky had so masterfully achieved in 1912. But the value of Wols' work, his personal stamp, is perhaps in the ever abortive escape, in the perpetual falling back upon himself, to the point of despair. Those who claim to be his followers or (like Mathieu) proclaim him to be

59   Maria Helena Vieira da Silva • *Normandy* • 1949

60   Jean Deyrolle • *Croy* • 1957

61   Alfred Reth • *Rhythm-Harmonies of Matter and Color* • 1957

62   Gino Severini • *Pastel drawing* • 1949

63   Jean Piaubert • *Ur* • 1959

64   Willi Baumeister • *African Picture* • 1942

65   Serge Poliakoff • *Composition* • 1957

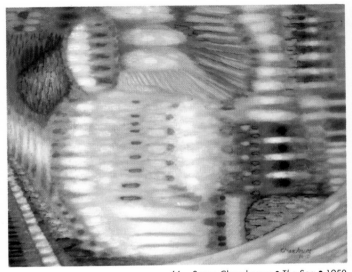

66   Serge Charchoune • *The Sea* • 1950

67   Jean Arp • *Olympia* • 1954

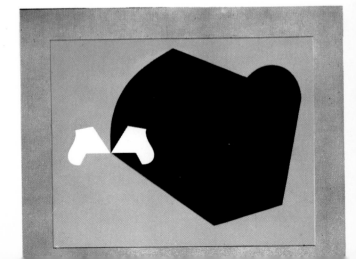

68   Pierre Soulages • *December 16, 1959*

69   Alfred Manessier • *The Ascent of Moissac* • 1959

70   Gérard Schneider • *Painting 69. E* • 1960

71   Jean Le Moal • *Roots and Water* • 1959

72   Franz Kline • *C. and O.* • 1958

73   Jackson Pollock • *Circular Shape* • c. 1946

74   Clyfford Still • *No. 1* • 1941

75   Jackson Pollock • *Frieze* • 1953-55

76   Fritz Winter • *Plowed Earth* • 1961

77   Jasper Johns • *White Flag* • 1955-58

78   Leon Polk Smith • *Prairie Blue* • 1960

79   Aurélie Nemours • *Angular Stone* • 1960

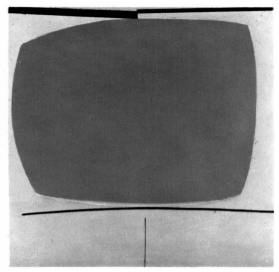

80   Victor Pasmore • *Yellow Abstract* • 1960-61

81   Ben Nicholson • *Still Life (Nightshade)* • 1955

82   Georg Meistermann • *With the Black* • 1960

83   Arturo Bonfanti • *Apparent Calm* • 1960

84   Nathalie Dumitresco • *Harmony in Yellow* • 1958

85   Ernst Wilhelm Nay • *Watercolor* • 1957

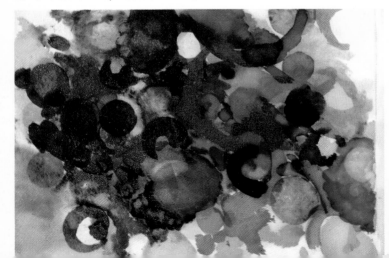

86 Jean-Paul Riopelle • *Trap* • 1948

87 William Scott • *Composition 39* • 1959

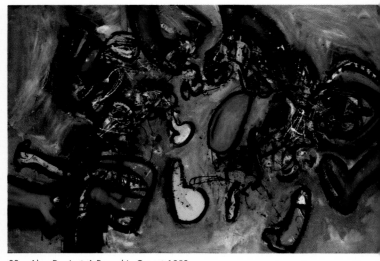

88   Alan Davie • *A Round in Gray* • 1959

89   Antonio Saura • *Louise* • 1960

the greatest painter of this century do not have his dramatic content, his authentic spiritual appeal. They have exteriorized it, and in so doing emptied it.

It was at about the same period that the quality of Vieira da Silva's work began to be recognized. She had attracted my attention a few years before with a series of small compositions — Lisbon landscapes or pure abstractions — which she executed on paper by means of the letters of a typewriter. There was a novel charm and subtlety about this game. But by 1948 this Portuguese artist had affirmed her linear and stippled rhythm in some very remarkable paintings. On the invitation card for her exhibit at the Galerie Pierre in 1949 I wrote:

"Little by little, embroidering her familiar theme, Vieira da Silva has created an irreplaceable art, a rare state of painting. Something is there which was never expressed before: a space without dimensions, both limited and limitless, a hallucinatory mosaic of which each element is endowed with an inner power which immediately transcends its own matrix. Every spot of color has a charge of pent-up dynamism, the force of which is proclaimed by the entire canvas.

"The beauty of the work lies in its channelized power, the way it bursts forth in slow motion, so to speak. A severe discipline, hidden by the easy play and the seeming improvisation of line and color, determines the slightest stroke of her brush which is never bested by temperament. Or rather, temperament in the case of Vieira da Silva assumes the form of temperance, order, orchestration.... Frontiers, frontiers, everywhere frontiers that delimit nothing, and that arrest no leap: what reaches beyond things is also within them. We need only wait. Such is the concept that I read in this painting. Someone was choking in the narrow spaces, and now he no longer chokes, even though the space is still there: the inner lyricism has overcome all limitations."

The years 1949/50 were fertile in revelations of new talents both in America and in France. The stars that rose in the sky of art, which had become cloudless, were so numerous that is was reminiscent of the crowning-piece of a fireworks display. In Paris alone, apart from De Staël, Wols, and Vieira da Silva, may be mentioned Hartung, Bazaine, Bissière, Lanskoy, Manessier, Soulages, Piaubert, Riopelle, Singier, Dewasne, Deyrolle, Vasarely, Poliakoff, Atlan, Mortensen, Schneider, Tal Coat, Szènes, the brothers Van Velde, Gérard Vulliamy, Estève, and Fautrier — soon caught up with and outdistanced by Georges Mathieu. This last, a master of calligraphic swordplay, was to inaugurate a kind of painting-in-public calculated to fascinate the crowds. Endowed with a lively intelligence and a remarkable gift for publicity, Mathieu has circled the globe with his "act" and garnered a harvest of success — a whopper, in the language of the people — beside which the most ardent of his painter colleagues look as pale as guttering nightlights.

The direct use of color from the tube onto the canvas, the violent application of paint in squirts and drips, no doubt produces novel effects, but a technical process does not necessarily change the spirit. Nor is it the rapidity of execution that confers style. At best, this can produce a popular style, as far from pure music as a popular singer who "belts it out." When one is seeking applause, one is sure to be the loser. For whatever histrionics are resorted to as a means of getting ahead, the results are bound to be dubious. This is the lazy way.

Art is a living thing, and a casual way of living empties it of its content, like a too rapid evaporation. This is why Georges Mathieu's theatricality is so far removed from American painting. There is all the difference between being and seeming.

Nonetheless, Mathieu is capable of charming calligraphies laid out with a very sure taste. The limitation of colors is skilful. Yet of his many talents, so lavishly exploited, the surest seems to be a talent for stagecraft — all Mathieu's canvases are stage shows. One wonders if he does not belong rather in the theater — at the service of the comic rather than the tragic muse. Nor is he truly modern, being too enamored of striking attitudes and masquerading. His real place is a booth at a fair.

It is not without interest to note that Georges Mathieu is the only painter in the world to have succeeded in setting up for himself a closed corporation of dovetailing interests. He has his mercenaries, his lackeys, his philosopher, and even politicians ready to vouch for him. And this, too, is a work of art, or at least of skill. We know what these solid fortresses, so logically organized, amount to: a worm gnaws at their heart which is their very order. And we also know what these intelligences having an answer for everything amount to: they lack a flaw. One is reminded of a woman too sure of her beauty.

I prefer chamber music to these fairground brass bands. And I hear many — strident ones — accompanied by howls, clamoring for a return to barbarism with all the appropriate convulsions. And this too is merely theater — I mean make-believe.

It is impossible for me (as I am sure it is for you) to reason otherwise than on the basis of a certain stage of civilization or culture. For this stage is a fact for every one of us. Can we lay aside reasoning altogether? Hardly. He who does not want to reason does so nonetheless, like Aristotle's philosopher who did not want to philosophize. Can we recover purity by reverting to a primitive state? Do we aspire to the purity of the primate? I prefer to believe that purity is something that must be attained, not something to which one reverts. Purity does not lie behind us. But perhaps what we are seeking is license, "freedom." There again we sink back into laziness.

Yet this simulation of the primitive, or the primate, was put into fashion. There are young painters, in France, in Italy, and in America, who compose a painting much as in the movies an actor composes the character of a cynical oaf, of a misfit. And this makes a lot of waves. So many waves that these false misfits, imitating one another like good children, fill up half the world. Which clearly brings out the fact that this is all make-believe, for if all these people were really "barbarians" (as the painter Appel claims) they would be in prison. But painters have never been put in prison simply because they paint. And that is why "barbarism" can freely disport itself within the limits of a picture frame without the slightest risk. And the "barbarian" himself is very careful not to go beyond this frame.

American painting, however, seems to be trying to go beyond these limits and to disobey all rules. In 1912 Severini had continued certain of his paintings right onto the picture frame. But American painters are at grips with infinite space without having had to paint the frame itself. This violent need of expansion is characteristic even of those American painters who have had almost their entire training

90   Kumi Sugaï • *Jishin* • 1958

in France, like Riopelle and Sam Francis. American painting of the past ten or twelve years seems to me to be characterized by a certain roughness pushed to gigantism, a certain self-destructive force pushed to monumentality.

I am thinking of Rothko, Kline, Clyfford Still, Pollock, De Kooning, Barnett, Newman, Stamos, Joan Mitchell, Gottlieb, Motherwell. Beside these titans, the painters working along the banks of the Seine seem finicky minor craftsmen — especially Mathieu, who is nevertheless the most spectacular. This is because all these Americans have a soul, a virile soul, which affirms itself as such. They do not indulge in exhibitionistic artifices!

I am by no means unaware of the fact that this same need for spatial expansion, for total expression by means of a brief sign, is to be found in certain French painters. But they possess the art of controlling their ardor without smothering it, which inspires confidence in the viewer. At this tithe paid to the traditional harmonies the Americans snap their fingers. One need only compare Kline to Soulages, Clyfford Still to Schneider.

While time speeds dizzily by, and the atom ushers in a new age, and the world's dimensions seem to be rapidly shrinking, the painters on the banks of the Seine continue to offer us a certain "intimism." I am obviously using this word in a broad sense, to designate a painting which speaks in a low voice and says many things. Paintings, for example, by the brothers Van Velde who, in very different styles, are such perfect masters of shading. Their art resembles chamber music, proud and at times hieratic with Geer, human and visceral with Bram. Bram van Velde's *Paroles*, a volume which appeared shortly after the war, bear a fine stamp of sincerity:

"The real world with its common logic pushes us toward catastrophe. The artist seeks in his work to free himself from this weight. Art is being transformed into politics, love into trade, education into an apparatus for stifling the mind. In the midst of such horrors, clearly only the dream within me has life. But how do other people live? — There is color, virginal expression — new, without a cage, without routine, without limit — a bath of sun and light. We must realize that nothing man does is of any value. The trouble is that people want to be paid. Only sick men can be artists. Their suffering pushes them into the accomplishment of deeds which reinvest the world with meaning. The sensitive man or the artist can only be a sick man in our civilized life, so full of lies. To think of art as a profession, how appalling! — Painting is man in the face of his downfall."

This confession is typical of a certain intellectual climate. Wols might have signed it. And many others. But how remarkable it is that works having their origin in a spirit of anarchy are nonetheless objects of order and beauty, that these children of despair bear upon them no trace of wound, and become for thousands of people "a consoling music!"

Manessier's work has this same quiet tone, this same intimate penetration which a certain farcical painter has too easily qualified as "false mysticism." An art of patient investigation and of probing attention can obviously not be understood by the mountebanks on the public square. But these brilliant jugglers, to whom fame comes so easily, are generally unaware of the fact that a walking pace, even a turtle's, may sometimes take one further, much further than the breathless running of a hare.

When all is said and done, the painters on the banks of the Seine remain painters of charm. Impressionism is not forgotten in their technique, and the climate of their works preserves a background of poetry. While, as in the case of Soulages, there is no lack of strength, violence is excluded. Between the most advanced of the French and American painters who can be compared with them, there is today a difference in climate similar to that between the French Fauves and the German Expressionists prior to 1914. Whether it be by a suggestion of atmosphere (Monet), by the analytical spirit (Seurat), or the studied composition (Manet), all the Impressionist virtues are to be found in the most recent French abstract painting. One has the impression that these artists must have made the rounds of the Musée du Jeu de Paume many times, admiring Monet's water lilies. Thus Bazaine, Germain, Lombard, Tal Coat, Bryen,

Manessier, Singier, Le Moal, Prassinos, and Vulliamy are recasting Impressionism with 1960 eyes. I mean eyes which are no longer fixed on the object but attempt to penetrate painting itself. This is an altogether different mystery, with something about it of the vicious (or enchanted) circle of the alchemists. Soulages and Schneider, with their fine ardor, do not break this circle but enlarge it.

The break occurs with the Americans. This is why we at first have an impression of imbalance, of loss of center, of absence of restraint. There is liberation here, hence a lack of measure. This appears as clearly in the works of Guston

91   Marcelle Cahn • *The Black Disk* • 1960

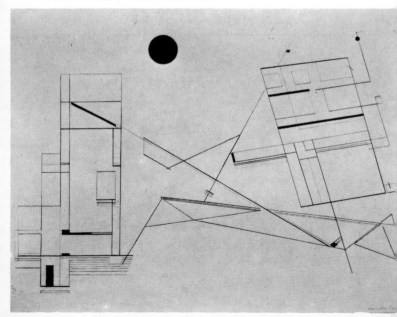

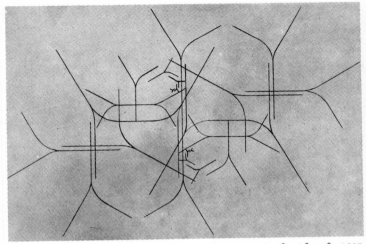

92 Max Bill • *Construction on the Formula $a^2 + b^2 = c^2$* • 1937

(who might be an Impressionist in his way) as it does in those of Joan Mitchell, who scrambles everything in a kind of delirious Expressionism. One may wonder if these deliriums really liberate. When the deep invokes the deep, though the cries become more and more strident they are never strident enough and end by not being heard at all; the violence becomes a kind of silence.

There can be no excess within the four sides of a picture frame, as I have said. And it is not up to me to try to find out what goes on in an artist's mind. It is the sign that matters; what he has to offer. And the only other thing that matters is whether I am capable of receiving this offering, of committing myself to it. I confess to experiencing great pleasure before recent works by De Kooning or Kline. But this pleasure does not exclude the altogether different pleasure I derive from works by Soulages or a Schneider, nor that which I feel before certain paintings by Vasarely, Mortenson, R. F. Thépot, or Glarner. I do not feed on a single dish, do not limit myself to a single cuisine, I am on no diet. I merely like it all. And so it is hard for me to understand people capable of liking only one thing — and all too often hating everything else.

Many artists of our day like to find justification for their work in science or in philosophy; the man of science and the philosopher increasingly scrutinize the phenomenon of art. I wonder if this "osmosis" is a healthy development. It seems to me that any truly original work stands or falls of itself, irrespective of the influences that have helped produce it. The fact remains that the Duchamp brothers were greatly absorbed in higher mathematics when they founded the Section d'Or. The fact remains that Mondrian read and reread Schoenmaekers, that Kandinsky was steeped in theosophic literature, that Arp is imbued with the pre-Socratic philosophers, Max Ernst with Freud, and Herbin with the *Farbenlehre*. Likewise, the America painters of the great wave of 1950 all seem to have read *Art as Experience* or at least to have heard of John Dewey. It is no secret that the French nonformalists of recent years have found the most solid support in Lupesco's theory of contradictions.

It is Zen Buddhism, however, which exerts the strongest attraction on both continents. It is clearly understood that in 1960s the abstract painter must be fascinated by the East, that he will dream of traveling to Kyoto, and that he will find his greatest delights in Japanese calligraphy. Who could complain if this would help to build a bridge between

93   Roger-François Thépot • *Drawing on tracing paper* • 1961

East and West? This type of bridge building is an urgent and essential matter, if ever there was one. But most of the time I see only paper bridges, multitudes of paper streamers thrown with a light hand to catch a flashy word. However superficial may be the contacts so far made, we must congratulate ourselves that some at least have been made, encouraged by the shrinking of distance. In America it was Mark Tobey who by his travels and sojourns in Asia established the first contact with Oriental calligraphy and revealed its hidden forces. The influence that his works exerted, (many of them very small in format) even outside

America, was comparable to that of the school of Hans Hoffmann, a teacher of painting who opened new paths for many young American talents.

Of all those in Europe who juggle (at times so heavily) with Zen Buddhism and Taoism, Degottex in France and Julius Bissier in Germany seem to me to be closest to the spirit of Oriental painters and calligraphers especially those associated with the calligrapher, in the Shiryu Morita, the editor of the magazines *Bokubi* and *Bokuzin*. The sole difference being that these Japanese artists use only black and white. The art of the spot *(tache)*, or *Tachisme*, the immediate expression of the spirit by the gesture, has assumed great importance in Japan these last years and the most advanced painters of America and Europe have certainly provided an effective stimulus for this growth. The works, for example, of Tomlin, De Kooning, Pollock, Tobey, Alcopley, Soulages, Schneider, Alechinsky, Hartung, Bryen, and Mathieu are very well known in the intellectual circles of Tokyo and Kyoto, where they give rise to a sometimes strained emulation.

Pollock and De Kooning were the two great names of American painting when I was in New York in 1950. For my part I added Clyfford Still to these, having been greatly impressed by a show of his at the Betty Parsons Gallery. A retrospective of Archile Gorky's work at the Whitney Museum, in January 1951, also impressed me.

I heard a great deal about John Dewey, whom I had not read. I was later to discover that the American philosopher's formulae at times paralleled Kandinsky's in *Concerning the Spiritual in Art.* "Art is a quality of doing and of what is done.... Art is an intrinsic quality of activity," says Dewey. And elsewhere: "A lifetime would be too short to reproduce

94   Julius Bissier • *Ink drawing* • 1957

in words a single emotion." The direct impulse here plays
as great a role as inner necessity, the inner urge *(innere
Notwendigkeit, innere Drang)* in Kandinsky's work. Dewey
speaks in deep and powerful accents. It is not hard to see
why American painters and critics were responsive to words
like these:

"A painting satisfies because it meets the hunger for scenes having color and light more fully than do most of the things with which we are ordinarily surrounded. In the kingdom of art as in that of righteousness it is those who hunger and thirst who enter.... Seeking, desire, need, can be fulfilled only through material external to the organism. The hibernating bear cannot live indefinitely upon its own substance."

To tell the truth, I had been forwarned of the importance of the painters of the new American school as early as 1947 by my friend Fritz Glarner (though his work follows a quite different direction). But I found the personal contact with Pollock and De Kooning to be singularly revealing in grasping of the meaning of their work. Pollock was a man for whom communication was almost anguishingly difficult. Despite his politeness he struck me as one who is as much a mystery to himself as to others, taciturn, reserved, with an undercurrent of anxiety. The superimposed network traceries of his painting, those inextricable labyrinths, seem to me to express the drama of a man imprisoned. A man for whom painting is the only way out of a situation from which there is no way out. He died, like James Dean, in an automobile accident, in the dead of night, leaving behind him as essential a contribution to American painting — and as isolated too — as did the actor in the realm of motion pictures.

Unlike Pollock, De Kooning was voluble, and seemed to like conversations full of leaps and bounds and unexpected turns. In his case, too, painting appeared to me to be the direct expression of the person. After his much-publicized flirtation with a distressing series called "Woman," his work has again become the most direct imaginable, a regular wrestling match with the canvas. Like Kline, Soulages,

Schneider, Hosiasson, Stamos, Sönderborg, Santomaso and a few others, De Kooning thus joins up with the art of the non-conventional sign used by the Japanese calligraphers: that is, with *Tachisme,* the art of the spot.

Tachisme is the art of creating a unique, inimitable accident: *hapax legomenon.* However, this accident, must be controlled, otherwise I do not see where the limit could be drawn between art and the perpetual fortuitousness of everyday life. For everything is accident. And perhaps all ephemeral gestures could be considered as art to the extent that they are the involuntary expression of our being. They constitute our art of being what we are. But this identifies art with life itself, and everything is challenged anew the moment human deliberation enters into play with the appeal to consciousness. Only when man assumes his full responsibility as a human can his work be considered a true expression of his being, an expression which at the same time become testimony, proof of existence or a possibility of transcending existence, an immanent transcendence. I wonder if *Tachisme,* an art of the spasm, as close as possible to a brief orgasm, is not at as great a distance from human freedom as, from an altogether different angle, the preconstrained art of totalitarian regimes. The one gives too much intelligence to instinct and confuses sexuality with eroticism, the other assimilates the ideal to ideology.

Tachisme seems to endeavor to achieve a deep cleavage between society and the individual, a cleavage which every individual can discover in himself. Indeed, such cleavages tend to resemble one another as a spot resembles a spot, as a cry resembles a cry. Thus nonformal or *tachiste* art leads to a kind of wayward universality, which quickly becomes as boring as Social Realism. Between the totally alienated man and the man totally integrated with society, there is a middle way, an extreme center which is alone capable of development and of deepening: it is the free culture of the man who is not *révolté* (in Camus' sense). This free culture leads to a personal, intimate conception of the universe which is expressed in the case of the artist either lyrically or geometrically. Such a culture finally, quite naturally takes its place in society, alongside science and philosophy. It is still the same alternative of opposition and of composition. This is laid down in absolute terms, for it does not seem to me that there is an opposition in art which does not sooner or later resolve itself into composition, and there is no composition which does not contain forces in tension — in other words, in opposition.

We might think of the situation in painting today as assuming the figure of a triptych. In the center panel stands Impressionism, which emphasizes the sensorial acuteness of the individual artist. To one side stands the American school, with which I would link the nonformal schools in every country. The third panel would contain the "constructionist" painters in every country. Thus I would describe the world of abstract art today as divided in spirit between sensitivity, uncontrolled impulse, and sense of structure; between style, unreflective expression, and harmony.

From the first glance it is clear that the Expressionist and nonformal wave (the terms *Tachisme, arte nucleare,* action painting are also used) is far in the lead. And why challenge the obvious? And why should this wave, helped by so many galleries, collectors, and propagandists, not take advantage of the natural head start furnished by all violent sensations? Yet this is not the only existing abstract art. "Constructionist"

95   Philippe Hosiasson • *Gray Painting* • 1960

art, despite indifference and at times hostility, persists with a calm tenacity alongside of the enormous group in the opposite camp. This deserves consideration. It matters little that the constructionists feel themselves to have been pushed aside by the main current, it matters little that their works do not create a stir, so long as they are known to a few. Johann Sebastian Bach was content to have a single listener. The situation of the unrecognized artist is, in a sense, a privileged one, since what is underestimated can only ascend; whereas what has reached the peak must resign itself to descending.

Also to be reckoned with are the surprises that an artist's development may hold in store. Hans Hartung, who before 1939 was one of the first *Tachistes* and a painter of pure impulse, has since become a stylist of slender, elegant forms, featherlike in their delicacy.

It is amusing to read a manifesto which some young artists published in Italy a few years ago, proclaiming "the death of style," and to note the resurrection of style in their work today. However revolutionary the artist may be, however hard he may try to set aside rules and principles, the very progress of his work will impose them anew. After eccentricities have been left behind, the inexorable logic of nature brings man back on his two feet and he resumes the march of his fathers, his heart beating time. I like to think — it is my fond dream — that certain very good painters I know among the most barbaric nonformalists will rediscover the art of caressing the canvas, of invading it slowly, instead of violently assaulting it in a brief embrace without the slightest preamble.

But I wanted to say a word about the constructionists. "Grandchildren" of Mondrian and of Malevich (as the non-formalists are the "grandchildren" of Kandinsky), they have

96 Maurice Estève • *Composition* • 1959

a heritage to squander or to use wisely. Vasarely, who is coming increasingly to the fore, has lately been encouraging the square to pivot in space, has transformed the trapdoor into a window, and the window into a shimmer. In Mortensen's work, Malevich's square becomes even more dislocated and acquires strangeness, and at times complexity with a sinuous line, unexpected in context, an obvious nostalgia for the descriptive order. Jean Gorin, for thirty years, has practiced pure geometry. His finest works are the very sober and bright reliefs he executed in 1934 and in 1960. Among the young, perhaps the most gifted is Thépot. His large gouaches show a true mastery in the orchestration of the whole gamut of grays. In America, Albers and Glarner are the ones who most brilliantly assume Mondrian's succession. Mention must be made also of George Terasaki, Leon Smith, Ellsworth Kelly, A. R. Fleischmann, Frederick Hammersley, and especially Burgoyne Diller who is the earliest in date of them all, but whose output has been small.

In both hemispheres, we also find some excellent female architects of the canvas. I shall mention only Marcelle Cahn and Charmion von Wiegand, both of whom knew Mondrian, and Aurélie Nemours, who carries on rather breathtaking explorations in the Neo-Plastic realm.

From the beginning, abstract art has been characterized by its internationalism, by what we might call its "stateless-ness," as befits a language which aspires to be universal (thus music in its infancy was Italian, French, German and Austrian). We have seen that prior to 1915 there were three centers of abstract art: Paris with Kupka, Picabia, Mondrian, and Delaunay; Munich with Kandinsky; and Moscow with Larionov, Gontcharova, Malevich, and Tatlin. A little later, during the First World War, the new centers were Leiden with *De Stijl*, Zürich with Dadaism, and Florence with Magnelli, Severini, and Terroruti. Then Paris again came to the fore, and Weimar became a hive of creative activity through the Bauhaus. Today the main centers are New York, Paris, Milan, Zürich, London, Cologne, and Amsterdam.

Italy, ever permeable to influences and having little resist-ance to fashionable trends, has excellent painters in whom

97   Fritz Glarner • *Charcoal sketches* • 1959

sensitivity dominates (Afro, Santomaso, Scanavino), nervous artists in search of nonformalist values (Burri, Mattia Moreni, Vedova), a brilliant colorist (Birolli), and also some constructionists who, here as elsewhere, do not enjoy the limelight (Reggani, Radice, Rho, Soldati). Capogrossi is an isolated figure. He has created a work based on a very simple modulus which enables him to approach all shores.

Switzerland is fortunate in having Max Bill, who has made Zürich the capital of "concrete art." This would be a considerable achievement if "concrete art" were not in every respect similar to what we are calling here "abstract art." But this is a quarrel over words. Bill's mathematically conceived paintings are well known, but Zürich also provides a home for the rigorously ordered works of Lohse and Graser. In French Switzerland, we find Baier and Bally. From a single theme dear to Max Bill (multiple small squares) Gottfried Honegger, who lives in Grisons, has managed to construct an arresting body of works by using only red or black with variations whose subtlety lies in the use of a barely accentuated relief.

In Austria we find Prachensky and Rainer, both *tachistes*, as well as Hollegha and Gustav Beck whose works fall more within the range of normal sensibility. Hundertwasser, well known in Paris, follows directly in the Viennese tradition of Klimt and Schiele. Also to be mentioned are Neuwirth and Mikl.

In Germany there are a number of abstract painters of Expressionist tendency, like Bernard Schultze, Schumacher, and many others. There are "uniformist" painters like Hoehme and Dahmen, and those who still compose on a theme in the classical manner, like Fassbender, Trier, Winter, Nay, and

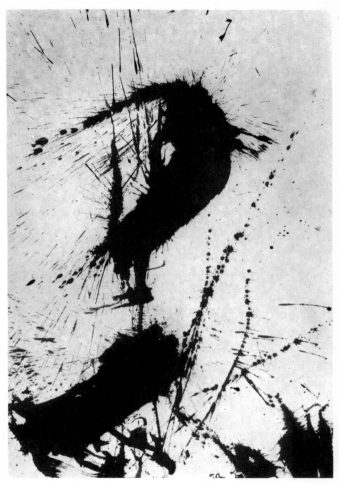

98   Mark Tobey • *Sumi I* • 1957

Ritschl. Baumeister, who died too young, has left no successor. He had been for a long time the most richly gifted of the Germans, his work oscillated with ease between constructionism and lyricism, between strong color and *grisaille,* between figuration and abstraction. A large retrospective exhibition which was held in Stuttgart in 1954 (one year before his death) showed the whole range of Baumeister's themes and the great variety of his techniques, revealing an inexhaustible creative vein.

In Holland we find painters like Appel, Ger Lataster and a host of their followers, who are all characterized by their addition to impasto. Corneille, however, does not share their frenzy. His more docile lyricism allows him to analyze his pictorial discovery so that we can share it. Bogaert, another unbound Prometheus, at times achieves fine effects of violence thanks to a sure sense of rhythm which enables him to dominate the liveliest gesture. Nor does he seem to believe, as so many others do, that a painting must make use of all the colors at once.

In Belgium abstract painting shows an even greater diversity of gradations. To list the names of Servranckx, Burssens, Van Lint, Mortier, Rets, Dudant, Van Hoeydonck, Delahaut, Leblanc, Verstockt, Vandenbranden, and Van Severen, is merely to set down isolated points which do not seem to communicate among themselves. Ann Bonnet, who recently died, was a very fine painter whose compositions combine poetry and solidity. This sense of poetry in construction likewise characterizes the works of Gaston Bertrand and those of Luc Peire.

In London one has the sense of being far from the Continent, and American painters are more appreciated than European ones. England is an island moored, not alongside Europe, as one might think, but alongside America. On the other hand, New York is closer to Paris than to London. Affinity is one thing (and here language counts for more than geography), flirtation is another. In any case, in the field of abstract painting, England is no more of an island than is the Île de France. Ever since the 1930s Ben Nicholson, has produced painting which is both rigorous and delicate. Strength and refinement are so intimately conjugated that it is difficult to describe his work without destroying its charm. Initially classical, Nicholson's work was recognized throughout the world before it was appreciated in his own country. This is proof enough of the universality of his work. England has other excellent painters: Alan Davie, Terry

99   Luc Peire • *Tessa* • 1957

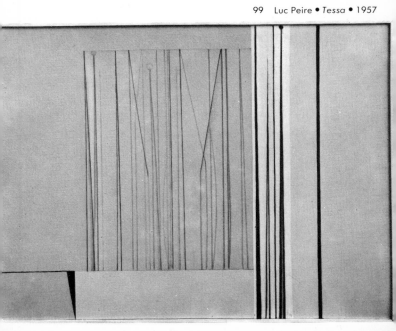

100   Josef Albers • *Indicating Solids* • 1949

Frost, Sandra Blow, William Scott, Roger Hilton, Avray
Wilson, Patrick Heron, and, in the realm of pure geometry,
Victor Pasmore. The latter's relief paintings must be
reckoned among the works most important in the Mondrian
tradition. "By penetrating ever deeper into the center of
things," Pasmore writes, "we can find the reason for their
self-determination; through the simplest structures the
essential spirit is revealed. The free spirit of modern art is
affirmed in construction, but it seeks the support of science.

To proceed from the center of things means that one is thinking objectively and at the level of fundamental things." An important group of constructionists surrounds Pasmore, but in most cases they are sculptors and their work falls outside the scope of this book.

Spain, which seemed to shy away from abstract painting, has brilliantly made up this lag within the past few years. It was in the *"Dau al Set"* group in Barcelona that Tàpies, Tharrats, and Guixart first revealed themselves. Later Millares, Saura, Canogar, and a few others founded the *"El Paso"* group in Madrid. All these names are now very well known outside of Spain, and there have been numerous exhibitions there also. These painters seem to seek austerity of vision and a dramatization of their material, and with these go a certain solemnity. Two artists stand somewhat apart: Feïto who is fond of chiaroscuro, and Sempere who is fond of geometry.

Around 1914, Portugal produced, an authentic pioneer of abstract art: Amadeo de Sousa Cardoso. It boasts today a group of abstract painters as varied as any other country. Mention must be made of Vespeira, Fernando Lanhas, Joaquim Rodrigo, Waldemar de Costa, Nadir Afonso, Gonçalo Duarte, Jorge de Oliveira, Vasco Costa, and Artur Bual. I find to my surprise that these Portuguese painters reveal every sort of influence save that of their great compatriot, Vieira da Silva who lives in Paris.

In Argentina, the *"Arte Madi"* movement has produced a host of artists, none of whom seems destined for the highest ranks. Muro, Sara Grillo, Ocampo, Lhito, Maldonado are good painters. Emilio Pettoruti, whose long sojourn in Buenos Aires has had a deep influence on him, has established himself in Paris since 1953, and has recently returned to the pure abstraction he had occasionally practiced in his youth in Italy.

In Brazil nothing essential, to my knowledge, has revealed itself in the realm of abstract painting. Brazil is represented in Europe by the Negro painter Antonio Bandeira, who for the past twelve years has been active in the avant-garde art movements in Paris and London, and was also a friend of Wols.

It is inevitable that in such a rapid world survey names, including important ones, have been overlooked, and for this I hope I may be forgiven. By lengthening the lists and going into detail I should have run the risk of committing the deadly sin of boring the reader.

After fifty years of existence, abstract art has its great classics and its minor masters, its tutelary gods and its adventurers. From the very first, however, it has tended to one of two extremes: Kandinsky's lyricism in the *Blaue Reiter* period, or that of Mondrian's classicism. A third and more central tendency has developed from both. Robert Delaunay was its first representative, and we might call it abstract impressionism.

For the past ten years it is lyricism (but a delirious lyricism, abjuring the lyre itself) which has prevailed in all countries. This vein, which is supposedly experimental, has long since ceased to contribute anything new. Painters young and old content themselves with mutually imitating one another, falling under one another's spell. So much so that this so-called "other" art — which even initially added nothing to Kandinsky save for a few thicknesses of paint — has become the commonest of things. After having steeped in vulgarity, one feels the need for a certain poetry, for the poetry of a certain slowness, for the beauty of calm works.

Were Rimbaud alive today, as young as when he proclaimed, "We must be absolutely modern," he would say instead, with the same boldness, "We must be absolutely classical." And he would add that it is time our century took its place in the succession of centuries.

My report on abstract art does not blind me to the qualities of figurative painting. I like Vuillard, I like Ensor, I like Kokoschka. Our century is sufficiently rich to treat itself to that painting too, including Surrealism. However there had to be a painting wholly liberated from dependence on the figure, the object — a painting which like music, does not

101   Hans Hartung • *Drawing* • 1947

illustrate anything, does not tell a story, and does not launch a myth. Such a painting is content to evoke the incommunicable realms of the spirit, where dream becomes thought, where the sign becomes being, where analogy becomes relationship and rhythm.

Who will venture a definition of modern man? Is he seeking harmony with his environment, or is he eager to detach himself from it? Is he more at home with lucidity or with the informulable? Does he adapt himself to new standards or does he rebel against them? Without answering these questions, may I be allowed simply to call attention to the fact that in totalitarian regimes the very formulation of such oppositions is excluded. This alone signifies for me that these opposites are necessary and beneficent, the very token of freedom. Every form of anarchy must be allowed to art, every form of license or excess must be given the possibility of finding a place within a picture frame. Art poses no threat to life, it does not endanger society. But when art is threatened, so is society; when art is made subservient to the state, life is made subservient to it as well. Today more than ever it can be said that a living art is evidence of freedom, and that freedom is evidence of life.

We have been considering an extraordinarily diverse number of categories of abstract art. What do they have in common? Is it enough to say that they are all specific to our time? Does this provide a sufficient link between the various categories? Leaving aside the wave of the innumerable minor *tachiste* and nonformal imitators, we find that abstract art remains bafflingly rich in its variety. This richness, which includes so many contradictions, would lead us to think that our period is a composite of a multitude of periods, that it has no character of its own. But multiplicity is itself a characteristic. And that characteristic is peculiar to it in an incomparable manner. The men of our time are multiple, diverse, and contradictory. As in no other period, man today is in search of himself, and art is the faithful image of this search. Thus the art of our time is one of the ways in which our age succeeds in being itself. Every successive work is a snapshot of our inner image.

But this stupefying variety reveals something besides a diverting individualism. It shows clearly that present-day man, in his search for himself, is attached to a theme, within which every artist discovers or conceals his own mystery. As I said earlier, in connection with Mondrian, his theme is for him the entire world.

For the artist of former times — and this holds true for the Impressionist and for the Fauve — it was the isolated work alone that counted. Artists were bent on producing a masterpiece, on achieving a perfect harmony. More and more, the artist of today expresses himself through a series of works. The work is a part of a continuity and tends to unfold in time like a concerto. The creators of this century are all producers of series of works, employing the resources of their genius to the same, ever-recurring, apparently inexhaustible theme.

In every other period of art history, the idea itself — the *what* — had been primary. Today the idea matters less than the way it is arrived at; it is the *how* that makes the work. This word brings us again face to face with the theme and its infinite variations. It is no longer a matter of knowing, of possessing the truth, but of approaching it, of heading for it unhurriedly, knowing that the road is long, knowing that the road does not end, knowing that the road is the end in itself. Art is not a certain sum of knowledge, technical or otherwise, but a reality in process of becoming, which reveals itself to us and eludes us at every step.

It is in this search — at times patient, at times feverish, ever moving and impassioned — that the art of today finds its intimate identity. And it is in the theme which is his own that every artist discovers, for his own use, a sum of knowledge, technical and otherwise, which will be his language, which will be his manner of saying — inimitably — what everyone knows, what everyone tended to be unmindful of for having seen it so often in the same rags, for having heard it repeated so often in the same tone of voice.

Thus the art of this century, in its very diversity, will undoubtedly appear to those who come after us as a homogeneous whole. But this simplified image will become meaningful only insofar as it expresses the commonplaces of the spirit in its own special idiom, in its own style. Through art, the incommunicable expresses itself without ceasing to be a mystery.

All the arts in this century have accomplished an immense revolution, as we know. We tend to know only this. The problem now is to integrate the eternal values in the revolution itself.

Revolutions renew the air, they do not change the substance of things. What is permanent adapts itself to the new climate.

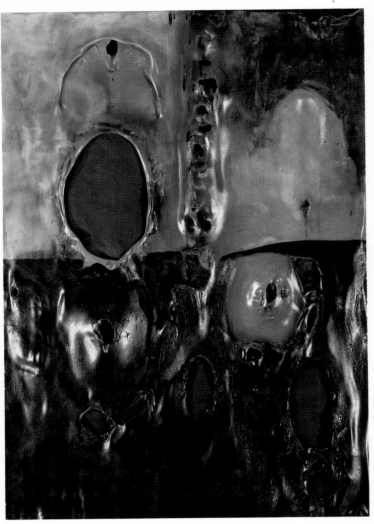

102 Alberto Burri • *Red Plastic Combustion* • 1957

103   Afro • *Villa Horizon* • 1960   104   Philip Guston • *Traveler II* • 1960

105   Burgoyne Diller • *First Theme - 35* • 1955-60

106   László Moholy-Nagy • *A II* • 1924

107   Mario Prassinos • *Painting* • 1960

108   Brett Whiteley • *Untitled* • 1960

109   Zao Wou-Ki • *January 6, 1960*

110   Edo Murtič • *Painting* • 1959

111 Joan Mitchell • *Composition* • 1959

112 Robert Motherwell • *Afternoon in Barcelona* • 1958

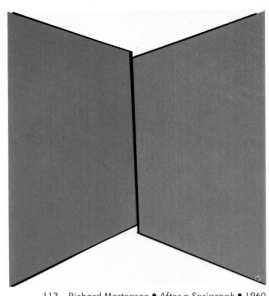

113   Richard Mortensen • *After a Serigraph* • 1960

114   Georges Mathieu • *Gouache* • 1958

115   Victor Vasarely • *Siris II* • c. 1954

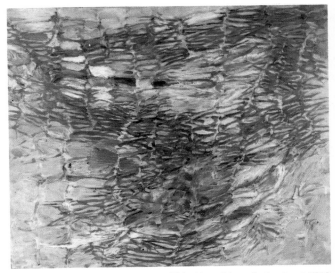

116   Hann Trier • *Springtime* • 1960

117   Conrad Westpfahl • *Colored Pencil VI* • 1960

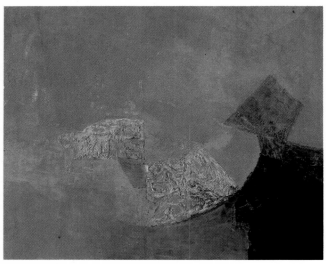

118   Joseph Lacasse • *Red Canvas* • 1961

119   Karel Appel • *Heads in the Tempest* • 1958

120   Louis van Lint • *Painting* • 1960

121   Helen Frankenthaler • *Svengali* • 1961

122 Gottfried Honegger • *Relief Study* • 1960

123 Richard Paul Lohse • *Rhythmic Progression* • 1952-59

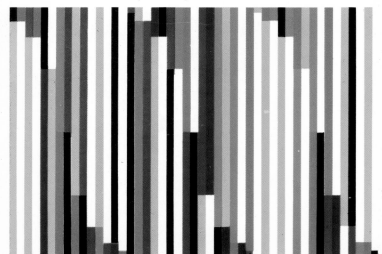

124   Lorser Feitelson • *Spatial Magic Forms* • 1952

125   Arpad Szenes • *Grand Canyon* • 1960

126   Huguette Arthur Bertrand • *Lul* • 1960

127   André Beaudin • *The Palaces* • 1955

128   Henri Goetz • *Pastel* • 1960

129   Wilfried Moser • *Painting* • 1960

130 Pierre Alechinsky • *Mr. Stanley, I Presume* • 1960

131 Gaston Bertrand • *Plaza Padro* • 1955

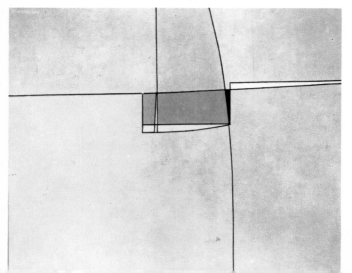

LIST OF ILLUSTRATIONS

● refers to color plates

AFRO
  b. 1912, Udine, Italy; lives in Rome
● *Villa Horizon*. 1960. Oil on canvas
  33^1/$_2$ x 39^1/$_2$". Galerie de France, Paris, No. 103

JOSEF ALBERS
  b. 1888, Bottrop, Germany; lives in New Haven, Connecticut
  Indicating Solids. 1949, No. 100

PIERRE ALECHINSKY
  b. 1927, Brussels; lives in Paris
● *Mr. Stanley, I Presume*. 1960. Oil on canvas
  43^1/$_4$ x 48". Collection Gildo Caputo, Paris, No. 130

KAREL APPEL
  b. 1921, Amsterdam; lives in Paris
● *Heads in the Tempest*. 1958. Oil on canvas
  44^7/$_8$ x 57^1/$_2$". Collection Dr. Pfluger, Thalwil, Switzerland, No. 119

JEAN ARP
  b. 1887, Strasbourg; lives in Paris
● *Olympia*. 1954. Collage
  12^1/$_4$ x 14^5/$_8$". Collection M. Seuphor, Paris, No. 67

JEAN ATLAN
  b. 1913, Constantine, Algeria; d. 1960, Paris
● *Untitled*. 1959. Oil on canvas
  19^3/$_4$ x 19^3/$_4$", No. 49

GIACOMO BALLA

b. 1871, Turin; d. 1958, Rome

- *Little Girl Running on a Balcony.* 1912. Oil on canvas
51$\frac{1}{8}$ x 51$\frac{1}{8}$". Galleria d'Arte Moderna, Milan, No. 10

WILLI BAUMEISTER

b. 1889, Stuttgart; d. 1955, Stuttgart

- *African Picture.* 1942. Oil on canvas
21$\frac{1}{4}$ x 18$\frac{1}{8}$". Private collection, Paris, No. 64

ANDRÉ BEAUDIN

b. 1895, Mennecy, France; lives in Paris

- *The Palaces.* 1955. Oil on canvas
44$\frac{7}{8}$ x 63$\frac{3}{4}$". Galerie Louise Leiris, Paris, No. 127

GASTON BERTRAND

b. 1910, Wonck, Belgium; lives in Brussels

- *Plaza Padro.* 1955. Oil on canvas
25$\frac{5}{8}$ x 31$\frac{7}{8}$". In the artist's collection, No. 131

HUGUETTE ARTHUR BERTRAND

b. 1925, Ecouen, France; lives in Paris

- *Lul.* 1960. Oil on canvas
35 x 47$\frac{5}{8}$". In the artist's collection, No. 126

MAX BILL

b. 1908, Winterthur, Switzerland; lives in Zurich
Construction on the Formula $a^2 + b^2 = c^2$. 1937. Ink
11$\frac{3}{4}$ x 19$\frac{5}{8}$", No. 92

JULIUS BISSIER

b. 1893, Freiburg im Breisgau, Germany; lives in Germany
Ink drawing. 1957
19$\frac{5}{8}$ x 25$\frac{5}{8}$". Galerie Daniel Cordier, Paris, No. 94

ARTURO BONFANTI

b. 1905, Bergamo, Italy, where he now lives

- *Apparent Calm.* 1960. Oil on canvas
18$\frac{1}{8}$ x 21$\frac{5}{8}$". Galleria Lorenzelli, Milan, No. 83

GEORGES BRAQUE

 b. 1882, Argenteuil, France; d. 1963, Paris

- *Woman Reading.* 1911. Oil on canvas
 $51^1/_8 \times 31^7/_8$". Private collection, Paris, No. 2
- *Violin and Pipe.* 1912. Collage and charcoal
 $28^3/_8 \times 41^3/_8$". Collection A.L., Paris, No. 3

ALBERTO BURRI

 b. 1915, Città di Castello, Italy; lives in Rome

- *Red Plastic Combustion.* 1957
 $49^1/_2 \times 35^1/_2$". Collection Henry Markus, Chicago, No. 102

MARCELLE CAHN

 b. 1895, Strasbourg; lives in Paris
 The Black Disk. 1960
 $19^3/_4 \times 25^5/_8$". Collection F. Graindorge, Liège, No. 91

SERGE CHARCHOUNE

 b. 1888, Buguruslan, Russia; lives in Paris

- *Ornamental Cubism.* 1927. Oil on canvas
 $7^1/_4 \times 21^5/_8$". Galerie Creuze, Paris, No. 46
- *The Sea.* 1950. Oil on canvas
 $19^5/_8 \times 25^2/_8$". Galerie Creuze, Paris, No. 66

ALAN DAVIE

 b. 1920, Grangemouth, Scotland; lives in London

- *A Round in Gray.* 1959. Oil on canvas
 48 x 72". Gimpel Fils, London, No. 88

ROBERT DELAUNAY

 b. 1885, Paris; d. 1941, Montpellier, France

- *Simultaneous Disk.* 1912. Oil on canvas
 $52^3/_4$" in diameter. Collection Mr. and Mrs. Burton Tremaine, Meriden, Connecticut, No. 5
- *Circular Forms.* 1912-13. Oil on canvas
 $39^3/_8 \times 27$". Collection Mme. S. Delaunay, Paris, No. 7

- *Rhythm 579*. 1934. Oil on canvas
  $44^1/_2$ x $57^1/_8$". Collection Mme. S. Delaunay, Paris, No. 40

SONIA DELAUNAY

  b. 1885, Ukraine; lives in Paris

- *Electric Prisms*. 1914. Oil on canvas
  Musée d'Art Moderne, Paris, No. 8
- *Catalogue cover for an exhibition in Stockholm*. 1916.
  Stencil Painting
  33 x $17^3/_4$". Collection M.S., Paris, No. 9

JEAN DEYROLLE

  b. 1911, Nogent-sur-Marne, France; lives in Paris

- *Croy*. 1957. Oil on canvas
  $28^3/_4$ x $36^1/_4$". Galerie Denise René, Paris, No. 60

BURGOYNE DILLER

  b. 1906, New York, where he now lives

- *First Theme – 35*. 1955-60. Oil on canvas
  $41^3/_8$ x $41^3/_8$". Galerie Chalette, New York, No. 105

THEO VAN DOESBURG

  b. 1883, Utrecht; d. 1931, Davos, Switzerland

- *Composition*. 1919. Oil on canvas
  Private collection, New York, No. 29

MARCEL DUCHAMP

  b. 1887, Blainville, France; lives in New York and Paris

- *Nude Descending a Staircase, No. 2*. 1912. Oil on canvas
  $58^1/_8$ x 35". Philadelphia Museum of Art (Louise and
  Walter Arensberg Collection), No. 11

NATHALIE DUMITRESCO

  b. 1915, Bucharest; lives in Paris

- *Harmony in Yellow*. 1958. Oil on canvas
  35 x $45^5/_8$". Galerie XXe Siècle, Paris, No. 84

MAURICE ESTÈVE

  b. 1904, Culan, France; lives in Paris
  Composition. 1959. Charcoal and colored pencil

$16^3/_8 \times 22^7/_8$". Galerie Villand et Galanis, Paris, No. 96

JEAN FAUTRIER

b. 1898, Paris; lives near Paris

- *Nude*. 1960. Oil on canvas
  $35 \times 57^1/_2$" Collection de Montaigu, Paris, No. 48

LORSER FEITELSON

b. 1898, Georgia; lives in Los Angeles

- *Spatial Magic Forms*. 1952. Oil on canvas
  Esther Robles Gallery, Los Angeles, No. 124

HELEN FRANKENTHALER

b. 1928, New York, where she now lives

- *Svengali*. 1961. Oil on canvas
  52×64". Collection Mr. and Mrs. John G. Powers, Greenwich, Connecticut, No. 121

OTTO FREUNDLICH

b. 1878, Pomerania; d. 1943, Poland
Linoleum print. 1937
$14^3/_4 \times 14^3/_8$". Private collection, Paris, No. 57

FRITZ GLARNER

b. 1899. Zurich; lives in Huntington, Long Island
Charcoal sketches. 1959
$19 \times 13^3/_4$". In the artist's collection, No. 97

HENRI GOETZ

b. 1900, New York; lives in Paris

- *Pastel*. 1960
  $26^3/_8 \times 19^5/_8$". Galerie Ariel, Paris, No. 128

JEAN GORIN

b. 1899, Saint-Emilien-Blain, France; lives in Paris

- *Composition No. 9*. 1934. Oil on canvas
  $34^5/_8 \times 45^1/_4$". Collection F. Graindorge, Liège, No. 42

JUAN GRIS

b. 1887, Madrid; d. 1927, Paris

- *Still Life with Pears.* 1913. Oil on canvas
  23⅝ x 28⅝". Collection Mr. and Mrs. Burton Tremaine,
  Meriden, Connecticut, No. 6

PHILIP GUSTON

b. 1913, Montreal; lives in New York

- *Traveler II.* 1960. Oil on canvas
  64 x 72". Sidney Janis Gallery, New York, No. 104

HANS HARTUNG

b. 1904, Leipzig; lives in Paris
Drawing. 1947
Private collection, Paris, No. 101

AUGUSTE HERBIN

b. 1882, Quiévy, France; d. 1960, Paris

- *Composition.* 1939. Oil on canvas
  18½ x 45¼". Collection Pierre Peissi, Paris, No. 44

GOTTFRIED HONEGGER

b. 1917, Grisons, Switzerland; lives in Switzerland

- *Relief Study.* 1960. Oil on canvas
  9½ x 9½". In the artist's collection, No. 122

PHILIPPE HOSIASSON

b. 1898, Odessa; lives in Paris
Gray Painting. 1960
51⅛ x 38¼". Galerie Flinker, Paris, No. 95

MARCEL JANCO

b. 1895, Bucharest; lives in Tel Aviv

- *Bright Morning Sun.* 1918. Painted plaster relief
  18⅞ x 27¼". Collection M.S., Paris, No. 34

JASPER JOHNS

b. 1930, Allendale, South Carolina; lives in New York

- *White Flag.* 1955-58. Oil on canvas
  52¼ x 78¾". Leo Castelli Gallery, New York, No. 77

WASSILY KANDINSKY

b. 1866, Moscow; d. 1944, Paris

- *All Saints' Day.* c. 1910-11. Oil on canvas
  37$^7/_8$ x 39$^3/_8$". Städtische Galerie, Munich, No. 16
- *Deluge I.* 1912. Oil on canvas
  39$^3/_8$ x 41$^3/_8$". Kaiser Wilhelm Museum, Krefeld, No. 15
- *With the Black Arch.* 1912. Oil on canvas
  74 x 77$^1/_8$". Collection Mme. Nina Kandinsky, Paris, No. 17
- *The Red Spot.* 1921. Oil on canvas
  54$^3/_8$ x 71$^1/_2$". Lent by Mme. Nina Kandinsky to the Musée
  d'Art Moderne, Paris, No. 36
- *Arrow Toward the Circle.* 1930. Oil on canvas
  39$^3/_8$ x 31$^7/_8$". Private collection, Belgium, No. 37

PAUL KLEE
  b. 1879, Münchenbuchsee, Switzerland; d. 1940, Muralto,
  Switzerland
- *Abstraction.* 1914. Watercolor
  4$^3/_8$ x 6$^3/_4$". Fondation Paul Klee, Bern, No. 25

FRANZ KLINE
  b. 1910, Wilkes-Barre, Pennsylvania; d. 1962, New York
- *C. and O.* 1958. Oil on canvas
  77 x 110" Collection Mr. and Mrs. Burton Tremaine,
  Meriden, Connecticut, No. 72

FRANK KUPKA
  b. 1871, Czechoslovakia; d. 1957, Puteaux, France
- *Disks.* 1911-12. Oil on canvas
  19$^1/_2$ x 25$^5/_8$". Musée d'Art Moderne, Paris, No. 19
- *Arrangement in Yellow Verticals.* 1912-13. Oil on canvas
  27$^5/_8$ x 27$^5/_8$". Musée d'Art Moderne, Paris, No. 18

JOSEPH LACASSE
  b. 1894, Tournai, Belgium; lives in Paris
- *Red Canvas.* 1961. Oil on canvas
  39$^3/_8$ x 31$^7/_8$" Galerie Jacques Massol, Paris, No. 118

ANDRÉ LANSKOY

b. 1902, Moscow; lives in Paris

- *Atrocities of the Reds.* 1959. Oil on canvas
  76^3/$_4$ x 38^1/$_4$". Galerie Louis Carré, Paris, No. 54

MICHEL LARIONOV

b. 1881, Tiraspol, Russia; lives in Paris

- *Rayonism.* 1911. Oil on canvas
  21^1/$_4$ x 27^5/$_8$". In the artist's collection, No. 9

FERNAND LÉGER

b. 1881, Argentan, France; d. 1955, Gif-sur-Yvette, France

- *Contrast of Forms.* 1913. Oil on canvas
  39^3/$_8$ x 31^7/$_8$". Musée d'Art Moderne, Paris, No. 20
- *Serigraph after a mural composition of 1924*
  16^3/$_4$ x 9". Galerie Berggruen, Paris, No. 30

JEAN LE MOAL

b. 1909, Authon-du-Perche, France; lives in Paris

- *Roots and Water.* 1959. Oil on canvas
  39^3/$_8$ x 39^3/$_8$". Galerie de France, Paris, No. 71

LOUIS VAN LINT

b. 1909, Brussels, where he now lives

- *Painting.* 1960
  118^1/$_4$ x 133^7/$_8$". Private collection, Brussels, No. 120

RICHARD PAUL LOHSE

b. 1902, Zurich, where he now lives

- *Rhythmic Progression.* 1952-59. Oil on canvas
  18^7/$_8$ x 28^3/$_8$". Collection I.L., Zurich, No. 123

STANTON MACDONALD-WRIGHT

b. 1890, Charlottesville, Virginia; lives in Los Angeles

- *Synchromy.* 1914. Oil on canvas
  Private collection, U.S.A., No. 21

ALBERTO MAGNELLI

b. 1888, Florence; lives in Paris

- *Sonorous Border.* 1938. Oil on canvas

57$^1/_2$ x 38$^1/_4$". Galerie de France, Paris, No. 50

KASIMIR MALEVICH

b. 1878, Kiev; d. 1935, Leningrad

- *The Guard*. 1912-14. Oil on canvas
22$^1/_2$ x 26$^1/_4$". Stedelijk Museum, Amsterdam, No. 22

- *Supreme*. Before 1915. Oil on canvas
26 x 38$^1/_4$". Stedelijk Museum, Amsterdam, No. 23

ALFRED MANESSIER

b. 1911, Saint-Ouen, France; lives in Paris

- *The Ascent of Moissac*. 1959. Oil on canvas
63$^3/_4$ x 44$^7/_8$". Collection Myriam Prévot, Paris, No. 69

GEORGES MATHIEU

b. 1921, Calais; lives in Paris

- *Gouache*. 1958
21$^5/_8$ x 29$^1/_2$". Galerie Rive Droite, Paris, No. 114

GEORG MEISTERMANN

b. 1911, Solingen, Germany; lives in Frankfurt am Main

- *With the Black*. 1960. Oil on canvas
18$^7/_8$ x 24$^1/_2$". Private collection, Germany, No. 82

JOAN MIRÒ

b. 1893, Montroig, near Barcelona; lives in Barcelona and Paris

- *Landscape*. 1930. Oil on canvas
61 x 90$^1/_2$". Musée d'Art Moderne, Paris, No. 38

JOAN MITCHELL

b. 1926, Chicago; lives in Paris

- *Composition*. 1959. Oil on canvas
37$^3/_8$ x 35$^7/_8$". Collection Galerie Dubourg, Paris, No. 111

LÁSZLÓ MOHOLY-NAGY

b. 1895, Borsod, Hungary; d. 1946, Chicago

- *A II*. 1924. Oil on canvas
44$^1/_2$ x 52$^3/_4$". The Solomon R. Guggenheim Museum, New York, No. 106

PIET MONDRIAN

b. 1872, Amersfoort, The Netherlands; d. 1944, New York

- *Apple Trees in Bloom*. 1912. Oil on canvas
  $30^3/_4$ x $42^1/_8$". Gemeentemuseum, The Hague, No. 13
- *Composition*. 1914. Oil on canvas
  $55^1/_8$ x $39^3/_4$". Stedelijk Museum, Amsterdam, No. 14
- *Composition in Bright Colors with Gray Contours*. 1919.
  Oil on canvas
  Collection Mme. Arp-Hagenbach, Basel, No. 28
- *Composition with Red, Yellow, and Blue*. 1921.
  Oil on canvas
  $18^7/_8$ x $18^7/_8$". Collection Mr. and Mrs. Herbert M.
  Rothschild, Ossining, New York, No. 41
- *Victory Boogie Woogie*. 1944. Painting with collage
  (unfinished)
  $49^5/_8$ x $49^5/_8$". Collection Mr. and Mrs. Burton Tremaine,
  Meriden, Connecticut, No. 47

RICHARD MORTENSEN

b. 1910, Copenhagen; lives in Paris

- *After a Serigraph*. 1960. Oil on canvas
  13 x $14^1/_4$". Galerie Denise René, Paris, No. 113

WILFRIED MOSER

b. 1914, Zurich; lives in Paris

- *Painting*. 1960. Oil on canvas
  35 x $51^1/_8$". Galerie Jeanne Bucher, Paris, No. 129

ROBERT MOTHERWELL

b. 1915, Aberdeen, Washington; lives in New York

- *Afternoon in Barcelona*. 1958. Oil on canvas
  $53^1/_2$ x 72". Sidney Janis Gallery, New York, No. 112

EDO MURTIĆ

b. 1921, Velika-Pisanica, Yugoslavia; lives in Zagreb

- *Painting*. 1959. Oil on canvas
  $39^3/_8$ x $53^1/_8$". Galerie Creuze, Paris, No. 110

ERNST WILHELM NAY

b. 1902, Berlin; lives in Cologne

- *Watercolor.* 1957
  In the artist's collection, No. 85

AURÉLIE NEMOURS

b. 1910, Paris, where she now lives

- *Angular Stone.* 1960. Oil on canvas
  35 x 45⅝". Private collection, Paris, No. 79

BEN NICHOLSON

b. 1894, Denham, England; lives in Switzerland

- *Still Life (Nightshade).* 1955. Oil on canvas
  38 x 50". Collection Hans C. Bechtler, Zurich, No. 81

VICTOR PASMORE

b. 1908, Chelsham, England; lives in London

- *Yellow Abstract.* 1960-61, No. 80

JOZEF PEETERS

b. 1895, Antwerp; d. 1960, Antwerp

Linoleum print. 1920

8¼ x 7⅜". Collection Naessens, Brussels, No. 55

LUC PEIRE

b. 1916, Bruges; lives in Paris

Tessa. 1957

28¾ x 39⅜". Private collection, Paris, No. 99

EMILIO PETTORUTI

b. 1895, La Plata, Argentina; lives in Paris

Harmony-Movement. 1914. Charcoal

17¾ x 22½". Collection Alberto Sartoris, Lutry, Switzerland, No. 26

ANTOINE PEVSNER

b. 1884, Orel, Russia; lives in Paris

- *Gray Scale.* 1920. Oil on canvas
  24½ x 18⅞". Galerie Claude Bernard, Paris, No. 32

JEAN PIAUBERT

b. 1900, Pian, France; lives in Paris

- *Ur.* 1959. Oil on canvas
$51^{1}/_{8}$ x $76^{3}/_{4}$". In the artist's collection, No. 63

FRANCIS PICABIA

b. 1879, Paris; d. 1953, Paris

- *Rubber.* 1909. Watercolor
$17^{7}/_{8}$ x $24^{1}/_{4}$". Musée d'Art Moderne, Paris, No. 24

PABLO PICASSO

b. 1881, Malaga, Spain; lives near Cannes

- *Bottle, Glass, and Violin,* 1912-13. Drawing with collage
$18^{1}/_{2}$ x $24^{5}/_{8}$" Collection Tzara, Paris, No. 4

SERGE POLIAKOFF

b. 1906, Moscow; lives in Paris

- *Composition.* 1957. Oil on canvas
$38^{1}/_{4}$ x $51^{1}/_{8}$". Galerie Creuzevault, Paris, No. 65

JACKSON POLLOCK

b. 1912, Cody, Wyoming; d. 1956, East Hampton,
New York

- *Circular Shape.* c. 1946. Oil on canvas
$23^{1}/_{2}$" in diameter. Sidney Janis Gallery, New York, No. 73
- *Frieze.* 1953-55. Oil on canvas
26 x 86". Collection Mr. and Mrs. Burton Tremaine,
Meriden, Connecticut, No. 75

MARIO PRASSINOS

b. 1916, Istanbul; lives in Paris

- *Painting.* 1960. Oil on canvas
$63^{3}/_{4}$ x $51^{1}/_{8}$". Galerie de France, Paris, No. 107

ALFRED RETH

b. 1884, Budapest; lives in Paris

- *Rhythm-Harmonies of Matter and Color.* 1957
$70^{7}/_{8}$ x $60^{1}/_{4}$". In the artist's collection, No. 61

JEAN-PAUL RIOPELLE

b. 1924, Montreal; lives in Paris

- *Trap*. 1948. Oil on canvas
$38^{1}/_{8}$ x $51^{1}/_{8}$". Galerie Creuze, Paris, No. 86

MORGAN RUSSELL

b. 1886, New York; d. 1953, Philadelphia

Sketch from a Notebook. 1912

Collection M.S., Paris, No. 1

ANTONIO SAURA

b. 1930, Huesca, Spain; lives in Madrid

- *Louise*. 1960. Oil on canvas
$37^{3}/_{8}$ x 50". Collection Henry Markus, Chicago, No. 89

GÉRARD SCHNEIDER

b. 1896, Sainte-Croix, Switzerland; lives in Paris

Painting 69.E. 1960

Kootz Gallery, New York, No. 70

KURT SCHWITTERS

b. 1887, Hannover; d. 1948, Ambleside, England

- *Merzbild*. 1922. Collage
$6^{7}/_{8}$ x $5^{3}/_{8}$". Collection Mr. and Mrs. Burton Tremaine, Meriden, Connecticut, No. 45

- *Small Home for Seamen*. 1926
$29^{1}/_{2}$ x $21^{1}/_{4}$". Lord's Gallery, London, No. 43

WILLIAM SCOTT

b. 1913, Greenock, Scotland; lives in London

- *Composition 39*. 1959. Oil on canvas
$59^{7}/_{8}$ x 72". Collection Charles Lienhard, Zurich, No. 87

VICTOR SERVRANCKX

b. 1897, Brussels; lives near Mechelen, Belgium

- *Opus 20*. 1922. Oil on canvas
$27^{1}/_{2}$ x $17^{5}/_{8}$". In the artist's collection, No. 35

GINO SEVERINI

b. 1883, Cortona, Italy; lives in Paris

- *Pastel drawing.* 1949
  $10^{1}/_{2}$ x $17^{1}/_{2}$". Collection M.S., Paris, No. 62

LEON POLK SMITH
  b. 1906, Ada, Oklahoma; lives in Florida
- *Prairie Blue.* 1960. Oil on canvas
  $39^{3}/_{8}$" in diameter. Collection Dr. and Mrs. Arthur Lejwa, New York, No. 78

PIERRE SOULAGES
  b. 1919, Rodez, France; lives in Paris
- *December 16, 1959.* Oil on canvas
  $63^{3}/_{4}$ x $44^{7}/_{8}$". Galerie de France, Paris, No. 68

NICOLAS DE STAËL
  b. 1914, St. Petersburg; d. 1955, Antibes
- *Football Players at the Parc des Princes.* 1952.
  Oil on canvas
  $22^{1}/_{8}$ x 30". Collection Mr. and Mrs. Burton Tremaine, Meriden, Connecticut, No. 51

CLYFFORD STILL
  b. 1904, Grandin, North Dakota; lives in New York
- *No. 1.* 1941. Oil on canvas
  $84^{1}/_{2}$ x 67". Collection E. J. Power, London, No. 74

KUMI SUGAÏ
  b. 1919, Kobe, Japan; lives in Paris
  Jishin. 1958
  $51^{1}/_{8}$ x $76^{3}/_{4}$". Galerie Creuzevault, Paris, No. 90

ARPAD SZENES
  b. 1900, Budapest; lives in Paris
- *Grand Canyon.* 1960. Oil on canvas
  $25^{5}/_{8}$ x $31^{7}/_{8}$". Galerie Jeanne Bucher, Paris, No. 125

SOPHIE TAEUBER-ARP
  b. 1889, Davos, Switzerland; d. 1943, Zurich
  Horizontal-Vertical Composition. 1918. Drawing
  Collection Jean Arp, Paris, No. 27

- *Watercolor.* 1927

  15³/₈ x 11". Collection François Arp, Paris, No. 33

ROGER-FRANÇOIS THÉPOT

  b. 1925, Landeleau, France; lives in Paris

  Drawing on tracing paper. 1961

  11⁷/₈ x 16¹/₈". Collection M.S., Paris, No. 93

MARK TOBEY

  b. 1890, Centerville, Wisconsin; lives in Basel

  Sumi I. 1957. Ink

  15³/₄ x 11". Galerie Jeanne Bucher, Paris, No. 98

HANN TRIER

  b. 1915, Düsseldorf; lives in Cologne

- *Springtime.* 1960. Oil on canvas

  51¹/₈ x 63³/₄". Collection C. Scheibler, Cologne, No. 116

GEORGES VANTONGERLOO

  b. 1886, Antwerp; lives in Paris

- *Composition XV Derived from the Equation*

  $Y = ax^2 + bx + 18$. *1930*

  47 x 24¹/₂". Collection Silvia Pizitz, New York, No. 31

VICTOR VASARELY

  b. 1908, Pecs, Hungary; lives in Paris

- *Siris II.* c. 1954. Oil on canvas

  7⁷/₈ x 11⁷/₈". Galerie Denise René, Paris, No. 115

BRAM VAN VELDE

  b. 1895, Zoeterwoude, The Netherlands; lives in Paris

- *Painting.* 1960.

  51¹/₈ x 63³/₄". Collection Henri Samuel, Paris, No. 53

GEER VAN VELDE

  b. 1898, Lisse, The Netherlands; lives in Paris

- *Composition.* 1951. Oil on canvas

  33¹/₂ x 31¹/₂", No. 52

MARIA HELENA VIEIRA DA SILVA

  b. 1908, Lisbon; lives in Paris

- *Normandy.* 1949. Oil on canvas
  $16^1/_8$ x $18^1/_8$". Galerie Jeanne Bucher, Paris, No. 59

JACQUES VILLON

　b. 1875, Damville, France; d. 1963, Paris
- *Soldiers on the March.* 1913. Oil on canvas
  $25^5/_8$ x $36^1/_4$". Galerie Louis Carré, Paris, No. 12

HENDRIK NICOLAAS WERKMAN

　b. 1882, Leens, The Netherlands; d. 1945, Groningen,
　The Netherlands
　Impression in Black and Gray. 1923
　$27^1/_2$ x $18^1/_8$". Collection M.S., Paris, No. 55

CONRAD WESTPFAHL

　b. 1891, Berlin; lives in Munich
- *Colored Pencil VI.* 1960
  $23^5/_8$ x $33^1/_2$". Galerie Raymonde Cazenave, Paris, No. 117

BRETT WHITELEY

　b. 1939, Sydney, Australia; lives in London
- *Untitled.* 1960
  40 x 72". Contemporary Art Society, London, No. 108

FRITZ WINTER

　b. 1905, Altenbögge, Germany; lives in Kassel
- *Plowed Earth.* 1961
  $53^1/_8$ x $66^7/_8$" No. 76

WOLS

　b. 1913, Berlin; d. 1951, Paris
　Drawing. c. 1947
　$4^3/_4$ x $3^1/_8$". Collection John Craven, Paris, No. 58

ZAO WOU-KI

　b. 1920 Peking; lives in Paris
- *January 6, 1960.* Oil on canvas
  $76^3/_4$ x $51^1/_8$". Collection Myriam Prévot, Paris, No. 109